Praise for
DIVE INTO INQUIRY

"This book is important! MacKenzie has written a powerful argument for inquiry learning to form the basis for twenty-first-century education. He offers detailed explanation as to why this approach is crucial in the current world economic climate. His useful classroom examples from his own experience and around the world will help any teacher implement new student-driven learning. The empowerment of young people to be agents of their own learning is the most pressing issue in this rapidly changing world and MacKenzie has created a blueprint to ensure this happens."

—Richard Wells, author of *A Learner's Paradise*,
Deputy Principal, Orewa College, New Zealand

"*Dive into Inquiry* has quickly become my favorite how-to book on inquiry-based learning. Filled with practical examples and solid structures that I know I can implement immediately, it has left me convinced that I really can create the kind of learning space that my students deserve. It is an approachable read that will change both your thinking and your practice for the better."

—Bill Ferriter, teacher, author, education consultant, USA

"Trevor MacKenzie has written a heartfelt book on student inquiry where his passion for growing a culture of inquiry and students feeling a sense of trust and empowerment are front and center. His clarity of message and practical examples of how to co-create this experience in other classrooms is inspiring. He offers fabulous examples of student voice, social construction, and self-discovery."

—Allison Zmuda, author and education consultant, USA

"Trevor MacKenzie has written a fascinating book, which takes the theory of inquiry-based learning and explores the practicalities needed to put the approach into successful operation. His passionate argument is underpinned by a deep understanding of the importance of feedback, pupils owning their own learning, and the need for clarity of outcome from the outset. I particularly like the graduated approach to developing inquiry learning. Too often, this approach fails because pupils have not been taught nor mastered the skills necessary to successfully undertake such an approach. I highly recommend this book for anyone interested in the power of pupil-centred approaches to learning."

—**Andy Buck, teacher, author, and founder of**
Leadership Matters and #honk, fellow of the RSA, England

"In *Dive into Inquiry*, Trevor MacKenzie tells the story of how he came to be an inquiry-based teacher and gives his readers tips on how to successfully move through the various types of inquiry-based learning. As teachers, we know that scaffolding is key, and this approach can help any middle-school or secondary teacher who wants to learn more about how to integrate this type of teaching into their practice. I especially enjoyed all of the sample questions that Trevor shares in his book—I will definitely be using them to help students reflect!"

—**Gallit Zvi, teacher, co-author of *The Genius Hour Guidebook*, Canada**

"Without action, the goals of 'genuine student inquiry' and 'personalized learning' will remain aspirational. Trevor MacKenzie's book offers practical and proven advice for bringing these ideas to life in a classroom. Your students will thank you for following his advice.

—**Jay McTighe, co-author of the**
Understanding by Design® series, USA

"As a promoter of Genius Hour, I was happy to read *Dive into Inquiry* by Trevor MacKenzie. The book fleshes out how teachers can make an entire class/course driven by inquiry, rather than just an hour a week. With passion, experience, and insight, MacKenzie explains what to do in the first days of school to change the landscape of learning for students transitioning from a teacher-centered classroom. He carefully covers everything a teacher and students will need, including how to co-create the course syllabus, types of inquiry, the four pillars of inquiry, essential questions, planning, research, authentic work and how to share it, and more. You will read and be inspired by stories of Garrison and graffiti, Eli and emergency medical care, Zoe the flourishing figure skater, and a score of other students who will bring inquiry in the classroom to life. *Dive into Inquiry* is a quick read, but it is meaty and worthwhile."

—Denise Krebs, teacher, co-author of
The Genius Hour Guidebook, Bahrain

"This is a book brimming with energy and idealism, full of insights and practical wisdom from Trevor MacKenzie, a teacher who takes student agency seriously. He provides thought-provoking examples of teacher-generated questions and the rich discussions that ensued. He is also keenly aware of the importance of moving beyond teacher questions to a higher level of inquiry in the classroom, where students are formulating their own questions. Inquiry, MacKenzie demonstrates, needs to be fostered if students are to regain their natural curiosity."

—Dan Rothstein, author of _Make Just One Change_, USA

DIVE INTO
INQUIRY

AMPLIFY LEARNING AND
EMPOWER STUDENT VOICE

TREVOR MACKENZIE

Dive into Inquiry
© 2016 by Trevor MacKenzie

These books are available at special discounts when purchased in quantity for use as premiums, promotions, fundraising, and educational use. For inquiries and details, contact the publisher: edtechteam.com/press.

Published by EdTechTeam Press

Editing and Interior Design by My Writers' Connection
Cover design by Genesis Kohler
Author photo by Sherri Martin

Library of Congress Control Number: 2016949996
Paperback ISBN: 978-1-945167-14-0
eBook ISBN: 978-1-945167-15-7

Irvine, California

CONTENTS

DEDICATION

To my sons, Ewan and Gregor,
for inspiring me to become a better teacher.

And to my beautiful wife, Sarah,
for everything else.

FOREWORD

For nearly two decades, I've been fortunate enough to work with current and future teachers in my role as a professor in the Faculty of Education at the University of Regina. For a number of those years, one of the major assignments in my classes is what I have dubbed the "Learning Project." The parameters are simple: students use primarily online sources to learn about any skill or topic that is of deep personal interest to them and then are asked to document their learning in innovative and authentic ways and to share their learning to the open web. Over the years, the assignment has resulted in my students taking on a variety of passion-based topics for their personal learning: playing the guitar, speaking a new language, even highly specialized skills such as tattooing and welding.

I imagine that few educators would disagree with the idea that school should be interesting to students. But my own students' reactions to being able to choose their own pathways for learning suggest that schooling rarely takes student interests and passions into account. Responses to the Learning Project assignment have been overwhelmingly positive: students are thrilled to have the opportunity to explore a topic that they are truly excited about, to be given permission to learn something they are passionate about, and to do it for university credit.

Yet, students' surprise at being able to direct their own learning tells a sad story about the common experiences of school. We know that student interests should matter, but changing the status quo isn't easy when it comes to such a traditionally defined part of our society and culture. Every year, we see scores of educational buzzwords, each heralded as the answer to "fixing" schools and the students they serve: innovation, data-driven, rigour, differentiation, competency-based learning, BYOD, grit, growth mindset, learning styles, engagement, gamification. While many of these pedagogical concepts have solid theoretical foundations, they are often misused, misinterpreted, and poorly implemented at best.

Inquiry learning is seen by some as yet another educational buzzword. While inquiry is frequently touted as one of the most important strategies for deep and engaging learning, teachers are typically ill-equipped to carry out real inquiry with their students and instead fall back on what amounts to guided research projects. In part, this is because inquiry learning, like many of the educational buzzwords above, isn't just an isolated approach to planning a single activity. Instead, it necessitates a major shift in the way we think about teaching and learning—and this type of shift doesn't come from a simple checklist or step-by-step guide.

This is where Trevor MacKenzie's work comes in. Trevor has years of experience leading authentic, deep inquiry in his classroom with both students and colleagues. In fact, his passion for inquiry is what led us to connect in the first place. In late 2014, I was preparing for a workshop to support teachers using collaborative inquiry, and as I often do, I sent out a tweet hoping that educators would share their own experiences around the topic. Trevor was one of the first to respond. He noted that he had done similar work with a team of teachers at his school, and he offered to share his process and resources with me.

Trevor's book solidifies and consolidates the resources and experiences that he has been so generous in sharing with me and others in the past. More importantly, while the book is full of practical, proven tips from his own experience, Trevor goes well beyond the checklist style inquiry that we sometimes see. Instead, he marries practical approaches with the theoretical and philosophical understandings that are needed to help educators in shifting their mindset around teaching and learning; he lays a solid foundation that is necessary to making inquiry a natural and fully integrated part of the classroom.

While the book is full of helpful ideas, a few key moments struck me as especially important. First, Trevor stresses the importance of redefining the role of the teacher in an inquiry-based classroom—perhaps one of the hardest lessons for teachers who, by and large, were schooled in very traditional educational systems where the teacher-student relationship is defined as a lopsided power dynamic. Trevor guides readers through the process of relinquishing control in the classroom in order to give students the freedom and flexibility to take control of their own learning, which is truly the first step in opening the pathway to personalized inquiry learning.

Additionally, Trevor delves deep into the idea of authenticity, another piece that is often missing from traditional schooling environments. He describes methods of guiding students in the creation of artifacts that demonstrate their understanding in authentic forms that go beyond traditional essays or posters, particularly relevant in a YouTube culture where people share their work and knowledge via video, podcasts, vlogs, raps, and slam poetry. As well, in the chapter titled "Public Display of Understanding," Trevor discusses possibilities for sharing student work beyond the classroom walls, whether locally or globally, a topic that is of particular interest to me due to my own work in the area of online footprints and digital citizenship. In a world where our children are initiated into the culture of social networking at increasingly younger ages, providing guided opportunities for students to think about how and what to share online should be (but often isn't) an essential part of any school curriculum.

From his first tweet to me onward, Trevor's passion for inquiry has been readily apparent, and this book is truly the product of his deep understanding of the subject matter. This topic has never been more relevant than it is today. The truly personal nature of inquiry learning is reflected more and more in a culture where we have instant access to an abundance of information and the ability to learn so much from the smartphones in our pockets. In many ways, inquiry learning provides a solid pedagogical framework for the often-casual methods that we use every day to learn about and explore the world around us. Perhaps, if we as educators can shift our mindsets and embrace this powerful teaching method, we can tap into the incredible curiosity and passion that our students bring with them to the classroom so that one day they will no longer be surprised to find themselves enjoying school.

Alec Couros, Ph.D.
Associate Professor, Information and Communication
Technologies Coordinator, University of Regina

Inquiry is the dynamic process of being open to wonder and puzzle-ments and coming to know and understand the world.

—Alberta *Focus on Inquiry*, 2004

Inquiry-based learning is a process where students are involved in their learning, create essential questions, investigate widely, and then build new understandings, meanings, and knowledge. That knowledge is new to the students and may be used to answer their essential question, to develop a solution, or to support a position or point of view. The knowledge is usually presented to others in some sort of a public manner and may result in some sort of action.

—Alberta *Focus on Inquiry*, 2004

Types of Student Inquiry is a scaffolded approach to inquiry in the classroom, one that gradually increases student agency over learning whilst providing learners with the necessary skills, knowledge, and understanding to be successful in their inquiry.

—*Trevor MacKenzie*

INTRODUCTION

I began my career at a school with a reputation for being tough—one with layers of challenges facing the educator every morning. We had a diverse student body reflecting the strong contrast between affluence and poverty prevalent in our community. Many of our students came from homes where their parents held jobs providing stability and support, enabling them to arrive at school ready to learn. But many students came from families who were less fortunate. Low-income and subsidised housing surrounded the school, two aboriginal reserves were located close by, and many students came from single-parent, income-assisted households.

For the first few years, I taught alternative courses that supported the needs of students who faced challenges no one should face—especially at such a young age. I provided breakfast in my morning classes so students could start the day with something in their bellies. I arranged work placements for students to gain skills and experience so they could perhaps find a job. Sometimes my students disappeared for days, weeks—even months at a time, and I had no idea what was keeping them from school. My mind wandered, and my heart hurt.

My colleagues and I were creative as we aimed to help our students. We were dedicated and tried anything from rewards to retreats to professional development. We tried anything we could learn or implement. We were all in.

To put this into perspective, two of our students became parents during their junior year and considered dropping out of school. But our administration and department hashed out a plan we hoped would keep the students in school and on track for graduation. The students brought their baby, a beautiful little girl, to school with them each day, and the students in our class all acted as aunts and uncles, each taking turns rocking the baby or helping the parents. Not only was it surreal—it worked!

During these years, I was also a mentor to students in whom I saw so much of myself—the underdog who faced an uphill battle without anyone to cheer him on. At other times, I was a father figure or a coach or someone who just listened. And I became a pretty good teacher because of those years and will always be grateful to the students who had such an enormous impact on me.

However, in spite of all we were doing to better meet the needs of our students, I felt I was missing something. I continued to ask the big questions I think all educators ask: *Am I doing enough? Am I doing it right? What can I change? What can I do to support everyone in my room?*

Ask yourself: What can I do to support everyone in my classroom?

#DiveintoInquiry

Not until about seven years ago, when a young man walked into my senior level English course on the first day of school, did I turn the corner to become the teacher I am today. During our time together, he made an impression on me to the degree that I would never be the same teacher again.

His name was Garrison.

Garrison was a good kid. He was polite, funny—charismatic, even. He was well-liked by his peers and good-looking. But like many students with whom I had worked, a bunch of obstacles stood in the way of Garrison's success in school; for example, neither of his parents had graduated from high school, and it was clear Garrison didn't see the need to graduate, either. He worked part-time to contribute to the family income, and this often caused him to be absent from class.

Garrison's older brother had been expelled from school a few years earlier, and he seemed to feel a similar fate awaited him.

The odds were stacked against Garrison. He would skip class and hang out in the "smoke pit," the public park across the street behind our school. He got suspended several times for various reasons. And he was disconnected from his learning. In short, Garrison didn't see the point in school.

But somehow, Garrison drifted into my English class. I say *somehow* because I've worked with quite a few kids in Garrison's situation, and most of them don't make it into the senior English classroom. Some take alternative courses, some transfer to another school or move away, some are expelled, and some drop out of school altogether. So Garrison's presence on the first day of class was a surprise.

I also say *somehow* because as I look back, several years after he has graduated, it seems fate was involved as I taught Garrison. I now pinpoint my time with him as the catalyst to providing something different for my students. Thank you, Garrison!

During the first few months of school, I watched Garrison reluctantly trudge through class. He read what we read, wrote the notes provided for him, and even did a few assignments. But nothing I gave him—no story or poem or novel—seemed to resonate with him. The teacher in me could tell that Garrison was just going through the motions of school and that he had become exceptionally good at it.

One day, I asked Garrison to visit with me. We sat down, had a chat, and with one small, simple, honest question, I began the journey to where I am today:

What do you truly love to do?

I decided if I were to get through to Garrison, I needed to include in our classroom what he loved and was truly passionate about. Through this conversation, I discovered his passion was graffiti art. In fact, he was a big player in the local graffiti scene and was a very talented artist. I asked Garrison if he'd be interested in reflecting on his art, his creative process, the challenges he faced when painting, and his motivation behind his graffiti. He agreed and, while I didn't know it then, what he produced was essentially a co-planned, inquiry-based learning unit.

Over the coming months, Garrison blossomed at school. His attendance improved, and his confidence grew. He began to share more and more of his passion for graffiti art, and we slowly built a body of learning that demonstrated a deep understanding of his inquiry topic. He researched the roots of the genre and artists who had influenced his own skills. He shared photographs of his art with our class in a PowerPoint presentation in which he described the theme of each piece and how his choice of colour and style supported his vision. He completed several compositions—some expository, some persuasive, some narrative—that provided a meaningful lens into the many layers of his craft.

And it wasn't just in our English class where Garrison was showing such promise. His attendance, engagement, and quality of work in other courses were also improving. It's safe to say that the highly personalised learning Garrison was experiencing was working for him.

Sure enough, Garrison graduated in June. And while I don't propose this graffiti unit was the reason behind his success, it stuck with me. Why did Garrison have to wait until his senior year of high school to share his passion in class and be rewarded for doing so? And why was he the only student to whom I gave this opportunity? Didn't all my students deserve a chance to dig into their passions, interests, and curiosities?

All students deserve a chance to explore their passions, interests, and curiosities.

#DiveintoInquiry

Since my experience with Garrison, I have been exploring how an inquiry model could be successfully scaffolded in my class, one hundred percent of the time. My approach isn't a single-unit, one-off experience. Instead, the scope is broader and includes all of the following:

- a mindful transition to foster student agency and support the shift in pedagogical models students will experience
- a collaborative journey through the Types of Student Inquiry that nurtures a gradual release of control over learning in the classroom
- gaining a grasp of Understanding by Design and planning for a performance task that demonstrates deep understanding
- honouring our students, their passions, and goals and tying them to the learning objectives of the course

This book is the culmination of the past seven years of furthering my understanding of inquiry and trying to make sense of how I can harness the power and opportunities it provides for both me and my learners. It is the result of many hours spent in the mess of uncertainty, not knowing if I was on the right path or if the changes I was making would yield what I was hoping for, all whilst trudging through the difficult feelings of trying on new and unfamiliar methods in my teaching. It is the end result of collaborating with colleagues, connecting with my Professional Learning Network (PLN), and soaking in as much as I could to enhance my teaching.

My advice to you, as you dive into inquiry, is threefold: first, think about where you'd like to be in a few years. Ask yourself what kind of a classroom you want for your students, and keep this classroom in mind as you move forward into adopting an inquiry model as your own.

Second, take small steps initially. Tinker with a unit you love or that you have seen provide meaningful and engaging experiences for your learners, revise it to incorporate some of what I propose, and reflect on how it went afterwards.

Third, continue to stretch your understanding of inquiry to best meet the needs of your own learners. I have had tremendous success both in my practice and with my learners. Keep your students at the heart of your reading of this book. Make sense of what I propose with them at the forefront, and go from there.

I hope you find what I have learned and implemented in my classroom as transformational and inspiring as I have. Enjoy!

TO ACCESS THE LINKS TO STUDENT LEARNING AND QR CODES INCLUDED IN THIS BOOK, PLEASE VISIT TREVORMACKENZIE.COM.

1

Changing the Landscape of Learning

Adopting an inquiry-based learning approach in my classroom has been the most meaningful change I have made in my teaching. The benefit of increased student agency over learning, the authentic connections we make to the world around us, and the twenty-first-century skills Inquiry-Based Learning (IBL) nurtures provide great reason to explore how inquiry can enhance what you are doing in your own classroom.

I love the definitions at the onset of this book. They provide a common understanding from which we can all begin to learn. But for me, inquiry goes beyond these terms. I see inquiry as the strongest method to create personalised learning pathways for all learners, a method that brings the curriculum of life into the curriculum of school. My approach is a scaffolded one that proposes a gradual shift—from the teacher to the learner—in control over learning.

To harness the power of inquiry-based learning, I begin each school year by laying the groundwork for a smooth transition for my students between other learning models they've experienced and inquiry-based learning. For many students, this will be their first experience with inquiry, and this shift can prove challenging for us all. So during our first weeks together, I focus on helping learners embrace their new role in our classroom.

My three big goals for these first weeks are as follows:

Gradually begin to flip control of learning in the room from the teacher to the learner.

The quicker I am able to empower the learner and make him more comfortable with the direction of our course, the more easily he will understand inquiry. Throughout my career, I have repeatedly seen students shy away from taking ownership of their learning. While this likely happens for a number of reasons, perhaps the most important is because we educators haven't been given the tools or knowledge to sufficiently support student agency. When we are equipped to aptly scaffold and support this shift of control of learning to our students, amazing things can happen.

Create an atmosphere of trust on which we can rely in the coming months.

As we travel through the Types of Student Inquiry and the tenets of Understanding by Design, we will unpack the Free Inquiry model, and our ability to trust one another will be of particular importance. Not only will trust help us journey into this new inquiry landscape together but, as many essential questions resonate and connect with each student, strong trust early in the year will pay off in the months ahead.

Begin to unpack inquiry and build the foundation for our learning for the year.

Students must understand the structure under which we will operate. They must be critical about the integrity and validity of this model and be able to assess the benefit and risk of working in an inquiry-based classroom. By doing so, students will be able to make rich and meaningful connections to their roles as learners in our class.

All of these goals are rooted in my teaching philosophy: **relationships first**. If I take the time to connect with every learner and get to know each learner's passions, goals, curiosities, and challenges, I am ultimately a better teacher. I will be better able to support their needs, deepen their learning, and prepare them for their future.

> ## Student agency begins by creating strong relationships built on trust.
>
> #DiveintoInquiry

When I first adopted an inquiry model in my classroom, I found those first few weeks the most challenging of my entire career. Letting go of previously used models was difficult, and I was uncomfortable in the mess of uncertainty. *Would the students understand what inquiry is? Would they be up for taking a more meaningful role in our classroom? Would it turn out as I planned and hoped?* I soon realised our first few weeks together contributed to the strength of our learning community, fostered the empowerment my students eventually embraced, and impacted the quality of student learning I would ultimately witness.

Two specific ways I helped my students make this transition were by co-designing learning and redefining the role of the teacher. Both of these focus on relinquishing some control over learning in our classroom and preparing students for the inquiry model.

2

Co-Designing Learning

I begin all of my courses by challenging my students to help me co-design our curriculum for the year. When teachers look closely at the learning objectives of our respective courses, we find quite a bit of freedom to decide what we can read, discuss, study, and perhaps most exciting for students, how they can demonstrate their understanding. All courses include a particular amount of "must-know" material determined by our respective governing bodies of education. My job during the course co-design is to ensure this must-know material is included in our plan. With this in place, we spend a few classes in small groups planning and designing the rest of the syllabus.

In order to communicate, I don't build a presentation criterion for this activity or assess the quality of the suggestions they offer. Everyone's voices are valued and critical to our learning, and I want the first few weeks of our course to create a tone where students feel they can contribute ideas without being assessed, graded, or judged. In my experience, this has positively impacted my classroom and helped create the student agency I hoped to foster.

To get the students going with group discussions and syllabus building, I share the following prompts:

- What topics would you like to dig into?
- Do you prefer class discussions or teacher lectures? Why or why not?
- Do you prefer learning alone, in pairs, or in groups? Does your answer change depending on the task or lesson? Why or why not?
- Do you feel visuals, videos, and other forms of presentations help your learning? If so, how?
- What role do you see technology playing in enhancing learning in class?
- In which way do you prefer to study a novel?
  - as a class, where we all read the same novel
  - in small groups, as a book club
  - individually as an independent novel study

- What forms of literature (e.g., novels, short stories, poetry, drama, media/cinema) do you most enjoy? What genres of literature (e.g., fiction, non-fiction, sci-fi, fantasy, romance, historical fiction) do you most enjoy? Do you prefer learning from a text or in a hands-on manner?
- If you had a choice, which of the following methods would you select for learning about a topic, and why?
  - research online
  - read a book
  - watch a documentary
  - conduct an interview
  - conduct an experiment or survey

- Do you prefer building criteria for assignments or having criteria laid out for you?

- If you could demonstrate your understanding in any fashion, how would you choose to do it? Here are some conventional ways:
  - writing an essay or composition describing what you learned
  - writing a creative piece
  - speaking aloud to me, a small group, or to the class
  - making a visual (*e.g.,* poster, Prezi, Keynote, PowerPoint)
  - using artistic methods (*e.g.,* painting, sculpture, dance, woodwork)
  - taking a traditional test (e.g., multiple choice, true/false, short answer, essay)
- Consider each of the following and how you would like to see each worked into our class:
  - What are you most passionate about?
  - What are your goals?
  - What challenges do you enjoy discussing?

After a few classes, I ask the students to share what they have designed, and we begin to work all the ideas into a single syllabus. We create categories and highlight big ideas, we identify competencies and learning standards, and we brainstorm performance tasks and create a "must-do" list. This list is different from the must-knows which I identify. The must-do list comprises items, topics, or experiences the students have deemed highly important to each of us.

Having co-designed courses several times, I've become pretty good at predicting what students want from their course. I regularly see options, voice and choice, clarity in assessment by way of clear and meaningful feedback about how to do well, and consistent structure and support as contributions to this process.

I then collate the student contributions into a single Google Doc syllabus and give editing access to group leaders. Together we hash out our very own, one-of-a-kind course syllabus. When it is finalised, we put it on a large poster and hang it in our classroom. We refer to it often during the year and periodically revise it to include new interests, thoughts, current events, or ideas.

This activity yields tremendous benefits. For example, I am always pleasantly surprised by the risks students are willing to take with one another after only a few days of being classmates. They share their interests and ideas openly, without hesitation. Also, the typical nervousness I have witnessed in class presentations doesn't rear its ugly head during this process. Because students are genuinely excited to take ownership of their course, their energy is evident in their presentations and helps build a common trust, leading to an exceptionally strong learning community supporting inquiry.

At the end of the semester, I ask students to reflect on their learning and experience in the course. The majority of them point to this activity as the impetus which created the trust and empowerment to strengthen their inquiry and build community in the room.

Trust and empowerment strengthen inquiry and build community.

#DiveintoInquiry

In my experience, this initial activity transforms students from passive learners to active learners. During the first week of our course, they see they have a certain amount of control over how we will operate in the months ahead. While I'm certainly not suggesting students be entirely in control, this is the beginning of a *shift* in control. And this shift is a great first step toward helping our students transition from a traditional teaching model to a culture of inquiry.

3

Redefining the Role of the Teacher

O nce we've started flipping control of learning in our classroom, we can move on to the next step of helping our students transition into an inquiry-based learning model:
Redefining the role of the teacher. As the school year progresses, students witness me wearing several different hats as I support them
through the Types of Student Inquiry and then into their own Free
Inquiry unit. A strong inquiry classroom requires I take on many different roles—teacher, coach, facilitator, networker, shoulder-to-
lean-on—at different times and for different reasons. In order for my
students to understand why this "hat-wearing" is important, I make
myself pretty vulnerable and open myself to criticism as we talk about
my role. Simultaneously, this conversation empowers students as
learners and helps them comprehend the type of teacher they will see
in the coming months.

The Inquiry Teacher: teacher, coach, facilitator, networker, shoulder-to-lean-on.

#DiveintoInquiry

As I begin this conversation, I write the following prompt on the board: *What does really good teaching look like?* I ask the class to consider the prompt for a minute and then discuss it in groups of three and prepare to share their ideas with the class after a few minutes.

I absolutely love hearing their comments during their small-group discussion. Their opinions are always passionately shared, their stories authentically heartfelt, and their desire to be heard almost tangible. Their discussions always take much more time than I anticipate, but I love letting them continue to talk and build on their definition of a really good teacher. I can almost feel a breath of fresh air enter the room as students slowly begin to realise this classroom, this experience, and this teacher will be different from others they have had. And with that, the shift of control in the room continues to gradually readjust from *me* to *us*.

When it is time to share their opinions with the class, I typically facilitate the discussion from the front of the room and record what they are sharing in a Google Doc. And I always remind them to be respectful and professional when sharing experiences about previous teachers who weren't, in their eyes, *really* good.

Even though I have done this activity many times, I am always pleasantly surprised by what students share with the class—not because it's unexpected, transformational, or mind–blowing—but because, in my experience, students want the same things from their teachers and their educational experience. As they share, I ask, "Why?" to pull more from them about why they believe good teaching is illustrated in their points. This simple question can lead to the most profound, meaningful, and personal answers from students that I have ever heard. Some examples follow:

- Be passionate about the subject, the students, and the school.
- Be fair, and don't play favourites.
- Be friendly but not a pushover.

- Be flexible and consider how busy students are when considering homework, assignments, tests, and due dates.
- Teach some real skills—things students will *actually* use in the *real* world they keep hearing about!
- Offer meaningful lessons and activities connecting to the students' world or lives.
- Make eye contact with students.
- Connect with all students, take the time to get to know them, and ask how they're doing.
- Teach and explain challenging concepts multiple times and in multiple ways (differentiation).
- Provide hands-on work or something to get students out of their seats, out of the class, or out of the school.
- Give praise or props—and not just for academic success. A teacher should find ways to celebrate every single student in the room.
- Understand student learning and how different students learn in different ways.
- Be serious—yet human.
- Have high expectations, but be supportive and realistic in striving to achieve them.
- Do some storytelling—but not *too* much.
- Give time in class for work and for students to get support when they need it.
- Have a passion for life.
- Be inspired to teach and "infect" others with your inspiration.
- Honour student voice by listening and providing options throughout the course.
- Understand students' lives and give consideration to what is going on outside the classroom.
- Provide many ways for students to demonstrate understanding.

Inquiry-based learning provides me with the structure and peda-gogical framework to be the teacher they have identified. As school progresses, I will demonstrate all of these traits as we journey through the Types of Student Inquiry and into their Free Inquiry unit.

Inquiry provides the structure and pedagogical framework to be the teacher our students need.

#DiveintoInquiry

Once we've listed their desired characteristics of a *really* good teacher on the board, I add the list to our co-designed course sylla-bus and to the front page of my teaching website, either as my header image or as a statement of the teacher I want to become. I use this as a reminder or "public contract" to strive to live up to these expectations. I try to make their input as visible as I can to demonstrate they have a genuine say in how we will operate in the course.

I also take a photo of the class's input and share it with our staff via email, Twitter, or Instagram along with an explanation of the dis-cussion. Students appreciate seeing that I am more than just talk. By sharing their thoughts with a genuine audience (the entire staff and my many teacher followers on Twitter and Instagram), I show them I truly value their opinions. Plus, I'm showing them I'll make their voices—and eventually their learning—public as often as I can. I firmly believe the more we make learning visible, the more students will understand the world around them and grasp that they have an important role in it.

The more we make learning visible, the more students will understand the world around them and grasp that they have an important role in it.

#DiveintoInquiry

4

Understanding and Assessing Inquiry

Once students have defined what *really* good teaching looks like, I shift the focus to inquiry-based learning and getting them to assess inquiry in action. While giving students a definition of inquiry and elaborating on it is a good start, adding an authentic example of students learning in an inquiry framework allows them to begin to grasp what our time together may (or may not) be like.

During this lesson, I want to accomplish several goals: I want students to witness the potential opportunities inquiry offers whilst simultaneously critiquing the inherent risks of Free Inquiry. I need to identify how the inquiry model will offer all of the opportunity IBL offers whilst removing as many risks as possible. Finally, I want to create a sense of excitement about the coming months whilst putting students at ease about the switch in learning models.

I begin by giving students the definitions of *inquiry* and *inquiry-based learning*:

> **Inquiry** *is the dynamic process of being open to wonder and puzzlements and coming to know and understand the world.*
>
> —Alberta *Focus on Inquiry*, 2004

> **Inquiry-based learning** *is a process where students are involved in their learning, create essential questions, investigate widely and then build new understandings, meanings, and knowledge. That knowledge is new to the students and may be used to answer their essential question, to develop a solution or to support a position or point of view. The knowledge is usually presented to others in some sort of a public manner and may result in some sort of action.*
>
> —Alberta *Focus on Inquiry*, 2004

To illustrate these definitions, I show the class a short video of the inquiry model in action. The video, *If Students Designed Their Own Schools...*, explores The Independent Project, a self-directed program at Monument Mountain Regional High School, a public school in Massachusetts involving nine students, a few teachers, a guidance counsellor, and the school's head administrator. This alternative academic program focuses on the four main bodies of learning (English, math, social sciences, and sciences) and runs for one semester of the school year. It is divided into three parts, all of which reflect inquiry in action: Weekly Questions, the Individual Endeavour, and the Collective Endeavour. These components shape student planning, learning, and assessment during their semester. Students decide on the questions they aim to answer, and these questions guide them throughout the project.

Before starting the video, I ask my students to pair up in order to critique it as we watch together. Specifically, one partner is asked to identify the opportunities he or she observes in The Independent Project whilst the other student is to identify risks observed. I challenge them to write down as many ideas as possible during the fifteen minutes of the video. Afterwards, the partners share their findings with each other and then with the class whilst I record their ideas in a Google Doc, putting all of the pros in one space and all of the cons in another.

I try to capture their exact words and then challenge them to go a bit deeper into why they identified something from the project as a pro or a con. I delicately touch on each of their points, calling on the contributors to talk about them and expand on why they included them. Initially, my job is neither to debunk any inquiry myths or misperceptions nor to celebrate any strengths or opportunities the class has identified. My job is simply to hear their concerns about inquiry, gauge their interest in pursuing this learning model, and provide them with the platform to share their voices. Again, this balancing of control in our classroom is so important in creating a strong inquiry community.

A strong inquiry community requires a balancing of control over learning between the teacher and learner.

#DiveintoInquiry

In the coming lessons, I will often reference their critique of The Independent Project as I begin to unpack the Types of Student Inquiry (Structured Inquiry, Controlled Inquiry, Guided Inquiry, and Free Inquiry) we will encounter and the structure under which we'll operate. But during this class, my goal is to address their points and share how many of the pros they identified can be accomplished in the inquiry-designed classroom I have planned. Additionally, and perhaps even more important for helping students be comfortable with our shift in learning models, I explain how I, as their IBL facilitator, plan to address the potential pitfalls they have identified in the video to ensure similar issues do not occur.

Try this activity yourself: Take fifteen minutes now to watch the video as a learner, identifying the pros and cons of The Independent Project. Divide a piece of paper in half lengthwise, writing *Pros* at the top of one side and *Cons* at the top of the other. Record your thoughts as you view the video, and pause if you need extra time to jot down more detail. And consider your own students: What would their concerns be? What would excite them? I love this video and activity, and I am sure you will, too. Enjoy!

Your notes may look something like these from a recent class discussion of mine:

The Independent Project Pros

- If students know their career path, they can begin to learn skills, content, and knowledge they will use in the future. They can get a head start on their future!
- Students work hard because they are genuinely interested in what they are learning.
- The learning experience is tailored to be more like a real-world workplace environment where students face unforeseen challenges, collaborate with colleagues, and perform challenging tasks (something **more** than just a test or exam).

- The program teaches students to be independent and have self-discipline. Students will learn to talk, share, and hone their public speaking skills.
- Students will collaborate with a broad range of people beyond their peers and teachers.
- The program supports different types of learners.
- The program allows for hands-on learning.
- The learning experience presents a level of positive peer pressure.
- Students are learning for their own satisfaction, goals, or passions.
- Students are completing highly personalised—and meaningful—projects.
- The program would possess less test anxiety.
- Students are answering questions to which they actually *want* to know the answers.
- The program promotes creative thinking.
- Students are more likely to listen to other student presentations than to the teacher.
- Students will be educated on real-world issues.

The Independent Project Cons

- Who graduates? What merits a diploma?
- How does a university assess an application from a student who completes the program?
- Are there gaps in learning outcomes? What if students choose to focus on a very narrow section of the curriculum of a particular course?
- Who gets into the program? What qualifications must they have?
- There's a risk students could give preference to some subjects whilst avoiding other ones.

- Can you "fake" your learning? With fewer teachers involved in the hour-to-hour function of learning, could you be lazy and procrastinate?
- Is it hard to learn self-motivation when the learner is used to the teacher having more control of learning?
- How do you transition between learning models? What does it look like? How are students supported?
- The learning style isn't for everyone.
- It appears there are no "experts" to teach students. Where do they find what they need to know?
- Student learning and how they spend their time is based on questions to which they're seeking answers, but what if students don't have any questions?
- Sometimes you don't know you are passionate about something until you've experienced it. Would this project close doors to certain possibilities whilst opening others?
- If students are looking for answers online, what constitutes an accurate and valid resource? What doesn't?
- What are the roles of teachers?
- Will you have the knowledge you need for pursuits after high school?

Students pull amazing questions and thoughts out of the video. They identify many rich and powerful opportunities available from adopting an inquiry model whilst pinpointing pitfalls and risks inherent in inquiry. Their concerns are completely valid. Nevertheless, I believe their concerns will be addressed through the structure of my course—the scaffolding of inquiry through the Types of Student Inquiry, the planning of learning using the tenets of Understanding by Design, and the support they will receive from me. As such, I encourage them to move forward with me to discover what inquiry will look like in our classroom as we unpack these big ideas in the coming weeks.

5

Types of Student Inquiry

F ollowing our critique of The Independent Project, I introduce the Types of Student Inquiry and begin to break down how these will shape our course in the coming months. Inquiry is most successful when strongly scaffolded, therefore I create an inquiry scope and sequence from the start of the course to the end. Simply put, we begin the year in a Structured Inquiry model, transition to a Controlled Inquiry, move on to a Guided Inquiry, and if all goes well, conclude with a Free Inquiry.

Utilising the inquiry steps in this order is a critical piece many educators overlook when adopting inquiry into their practice. Many teachers get so inspired by the Free Inquiry process I share at conferences, as well as the essential questions students ask and the demonstrations of learning students produce, they have their students dive right into Free Inquiry when they return to teaching. In my experience, without flipping control in the classroom, empowering student learning, and scaffolding with the Types of Student Inquiry, students will not feel as confident, supported, or empowered through their inquiry journey.

Without the Types of Student Inquiry, students will not feel as confident, supported, or empowered through their inquiry journey.

#DiveintoInquiry

Students should feel connected to their learning, certain about how to plan their inquiry, and comfortable with its responsibility. The Types of Student Inquiry help me assure these occur. Just as I begin the course with a gradual release of control of our learning, the Types of Student Inquiry gradually introduces the inquiry process.

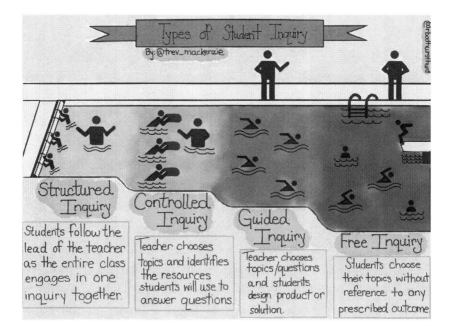

Structured Inquiry: students follow the lead of the teacher as the entire class engages in one inquiry together.

In the shallow end of the Types of Student Inquiry pool, Structured Inquiry gives the teacher complete control of the essential question, the resources students will use to create understanding, specific learning evidence, and the performance task students will complete to demonstrate their understanding.

During Structured Inquiry, all students embark in deepening their understanding of the same essential question using the same resource or resources. Further, they all demonstrate their understanding in a common fashion. Control of learning is in the hands of the teacher. The teacher's aim is to help learners strengthen their understanding of the various elements of inquiry, such as creating an essential question, selecting strong resources, conducting research, creating learning evidence, and completing an authentic piece.

Controlled Inquiry: the teacher chooses topics and identifies the resources students will use to answer the questions.

In Controlled Inquiry, the teacher provides several essential questions for students to unpack. Students deepen their understanding by using several resources predetermined by the teacher to provide valuable context and rich meaning relative to the essential questions. Students will demonstrate their learning by a common performance task.

In Controlled Inquiry, agency over learning shifts more to the student as they are given more choice over the essential question and resources they will explore. I suggest providing three to five essential questions that you are confident meet the demands of the course and will engage your learners. Further, for each essential question, have two or three resources selected for students to deepen their understanding of their inquiry.

Guided Inquiry: the teacher chooses topics and questions, and students design the product or solution.

In Guided Inquiry, the teacher further empowers student agency by providing a single essential question (perhaps several) for students to study, whilst the students select the resources they will use to research their answers and choose how they will demonstrate understanding. Student agency over learning comes through this selection of resources and performance task.

Free Inquiry: the students choose their topics without reference to any prescribed outcome.

In the deep end of the Types of Student Inquiry pool, Free Inquiry allows students, with the support and facilitation of the teacher, to construct their own essential question, research a wide array of resources, customise their learning evidence, and design their own performance task to demonstrate their learning.

To provide some context, during the Free Inquiry unit in my classroom, I typically have thirty students learning about thirty different essential questions. It is possible that each of those students could be seeking information from different resources as they plan how to demonstrate their learning in unique ways.

Understandably, this seems overwhelming; however, it is important to note by the time we get to the Free Inquiry unit in the course, we have spent a considerable amount of time unpacking inquiry and critically reflecting on the design of each unit of study—each Type of Student Inquiry. Students have discussed and answered essential questions and drafted their own. They have been introduced to a variety of online research databases and assessed their usability and validity. They have utilised learning evidence throughout the inquiry process and have demonstrated their learning as a summative performance task in a number of ways. By the time students encounter Free Inquiry, they have a variety of tools to help them successfully curb the perceived risks of inquiry. The design of the course, by way of the Types of Student Inquiry outlined above, is scaffolded to support this final unit of Free Inquiry.

I love the Types of Student Inquiry framework because it provides a number of advantages to prepare my students for success in the course whilst simultaneously fostering a learning community to deepen understanding and nurture student agency.

THE MUST–KNOW CONTENT COMES BEFORE FREE INQUIRY

As stated in the Course Syllabus chapter, each course contains a certain amount of must-know content. I weave these learning objectives into everything we do throughout the year. The Types of Student Inquiry provides me with the structure I need to ensure the must-know content gets covered in the inquiry-based learning classroom. For example, I frontload this content in the Structured, Controlled, and Guided units so by the time we get to Free Inquiry, I know my students have created a deep understanding of our course's learning objectives. But the Free Inquiry unit isn't exempt from the course's learning objectives. As you will see in the Free Inquiry Proposal section, students will co-design their Free Inquiry unit with an eye on how their plan meets the learning standards of our course. Until then, I use the scaffolding provided by the Types of Student Inquiry to ensure students learn the specific concepts and content demanded in the course.

UTILISING THE TENETS OF UNDERSTANDING BY DESIGN

Understanding By Design (*UbD*™), authored by Jay McTighe and Grant Wiggins, is a planning process and structure guide to curriculum, assessment, and instruction. I have found this to be the most powerful and supportive framework for planning my units of study. There are two key ideas in the book:

1. Focus on teaching and assessing for understanding and learning transfer.
2. Design the curriculum "backward" from those ends.

UbD is the most powerful and supportive framework for planning units of study.

#DiveintoInquiry

Also referred to as Backwards Design, *Understanding by Design* calls for educators to plan with the end in mind by first clarifying the learning they seek and identifying the learning results. For this to be achieved, we must think about the assessment evidence needed to show students have achieved the desired learning. We then shift planning toward the teaching, learning activities, and resources to scaffold understanding and help students achieve the goals.

I love *Understanding by Design* because it makes sense. My inquiry classroom is deeply rooted in the work of McTighe and Wiggins, as we'll further see when we get to the Essential Questions chapter. If the performance task students will use to demonstrate understanding is an essay, we need to plan our unit from this end. In order to write a strong essay, students need to accomplish many smaller, yet pivotal tasks leading up to this performance task.

Working backwards from the performance task, I ask my students to complete the following:

- a rough draft essay combined with an editing process
- an essay outline
- processing and reflection activities
- research and note taking
- accessing prior knowledge

These provide the knowledge base and preparation necessary to execute the essay performance task.

Teaching my students Understanding by Design not only strengthens their ability to plan, initiate, revise, and execute their inquiry successfully but also propels them toward greater achievement of a performance task they can be proud of. By demonstrating how a performance task is scaffolded through formative assessments and how rich and meaningful feedback leads to a building of skills, I have witnessed that students become more in tune with what they can do to improve their performance task and enrich their understanding.

> Teaching my students UbD propels them toward a greater achievement of a performance task they can be proud of.
>
> #DiveintoInquiry

I also love that the UbD framework can be applied to any future unit-planning or goal-setting situation. In each Type of Student Inquiry, I outline the unit from beginning to end, using a common language each time to help deepen the students' grasp of Understanding by Design.

As we transition from Structured through Controlled to Guided Inquiry, we constantly reflect on more than the essential question and resources we are studying. We look at the design of the unit and how I am scaffolding toward each student gaining a strong understanding of our question which they will demonstrate in their summative assessment. We discuss how particular tools to capture evidence of learning support particular demonstrations of learning. We assess which research methods and databases meet our needs and the merits of each. Essentially, we are learning two things simultaneously: We are learning about our essential question and trying to answer it whilst learning a strong structure applicable to setting a goal and working to achieve it. The marrying of inquiry and the tenets of Understanding by Design allow this rich learning opportunity.

Twenty-First-Century Learners

The Types of Student Inquiry allow me to touch on many soft skills students need to navigate their constantly changing world—curiosity, creativity, initiative, multi-disciplinary thinking, and empathy. These skills are vastly different from certain hallmarks of the traditional classroom, such as memorization of facts and performance of routine tasks, which are becoming less and less important. Add in growth mind-set, grit, and character, and we begin to see more clearly how inquiry-based learning and the Types of Student Inquiry provide a structure to best prepare students for the challenges they will face in the future.

Let's look at a few working models of the Types of Student Inquiry unfolded in a variety of disciplines. Each example breaks down inquiry and highlights the main components of each unit.

The inquiry student is curious, creative, shows initiative and multi-disciplinary thinking, is empathetic, and exhibits a growth mind-set, grit, and character.

#DiveintoInquiry

Type of Student Inquiry: Structured

COURSE: SENIOR ENGLISH

ESSENTIAL QUESTION: How many personal values must one compromise to live in society?

RESOURCE: Read a predetermined novel exploring this essential question (*e.g.,* Jon Krakauer's *Into the Wild*).

LEARNING EVIDENCE:

- Note-taking
- T-chart tracking passages from the novel reflecting this essential question on one side and student reflections and explanations about how the passage illustrates the essential question on the other side
- Rough draft
- Editing process

PERFORMANCE TASK: Create a literary analysis essay.

COURSE: JUNIOR MATH

ESSENTIAL QUESTION: What time in the morning must a ship, anchored in a harbour, set sail to avoid being beached at low tide?

RESOURCE:

- Graph knowledge by way of a lesson, online tutorial, or interview.
- Find or create a video demonstrating the tidal process.
- Find images depicting the setting and imagery of the tidal process.

LEARNING EVIDENCE:

- Graphs
- Diagrams
- Notes of equations and attempts at solving the problem

PERFORMANCE TASK: Create a tidal schedule chart for our coastal community.

Type of Student Inquiry: Controlled

COURSE: JUNIOR SCIENCE

ESSENTIAL QUESTION: What is cell division and why is mitosis important for life to continue?

RESOURCE: Students select a specific section of the science textbook to answer the essential question.

Learning Evidence:
- Notes summarizing the big ideas and must-know details
- A script to help in the recording of the video
- Images
- Graphs
- Diagrams

PERFORMANCE TASK: Create a video using *Explain Everything.*

COURSE: JUNIOR OR SENIOR SPANISH

ESSENTIAL QUESTION: What characteristics define a culture?

RESOURCE: Students research a variety of predetermined websites, articles, brochures, and books to obtain information about a selected Spanish-speaking nation.

LEARNING EVIDENCE:
- Summarizing notes
- Images
- Poster plan and outline
- Draft of text for the various sections of the poster or booth

PERFORMANCE TASK: Create a poster or information booth.

Type of Student Inquiry: Guided

COURSE: SENIOR HISTORY

Essential Question: How can the events of the past help us better understand the world today?

Resource: Students choose one of the following:

- Website
- Online article
- Newspaper article
- Magazine article

Learning Evidence:

- Notes summarizing the big ideas and must-know details
- A script to help in the recording of the video
- Images
- Graphs
- Diagrams

Performance Task: Students choose one of the following:

- Video made using Explain Everything
- Google slides, Keynote, PowerPoint, or Prezi
- Poster or information booth

COURSE: SENIOR BIOLOGY, PHYSICS, AND CHEMISTRY

ESSENTIAL QUESTION: What is the importance of the scientific method?

RESOURCE: Students select one of several case studies provided and explore the scientific method as they unpack it.

LEARNING EVIDENCE:

- Outline of objective or purpose
- Materials used
- Procedure
- Prelab question, data collection, and table
- Post lab questions
- Discussion
- Conclusion

PERFORMANCE TASK: Create a written lab report.

COURSE: SENIOR FOODS AND NUTRITION

ESSENTIAL QUESTION: Given a fixed budget, is healthy eating affordable?

RESOURCE: Students choose one of the following:

- Website
- Video
- Cookbook

LEARNING EVIDENCE:

- Notes summarizing the research
- Recipe
- Receipts
- Notes about attempts to prepare the dish

PERFORMANCE TASK: Using only ten dollars, prepare a meal for four students.

PLANNING AN INQUIRY UNIT OF YOUR OWN

Start with a Structured Inquiry unit.

It's always easier to focus on a single essential question, resource, learning evidence, and performance task. Start easy. Reflect. Try it again.

Start with a topic or unit you have taught before.

Use a lesson or unit you have taught before to take the dip into inquiry. Choose one that really resonated with your learners. Reframe the lesson to begin with a powerful essential question. When you are familiar and comfortable with the material, you'll most likely be more comfortable with reframing and getting to the performance task.

Start small.

You do not need to redesign your whole year or even an entire unit of study. Start small. Begin by adding essential questions to your lessons. This single change to your practice will lead to a future of powerful and deep inquiry roots. Model these questions first. Demonstrate how they can lead to a deepening of learning. Teach students to ask essential questions of their own. And finally, use these essential questions to guide activities, lessons, resources, and performance tasks.

Start with what you know, start small,
and start with the end in mind.

#DiveintoInquiry

Start with the end in mind.

Always show your learners the target for which they're aiming before you begin the journey through learning together. As students unpack information and create understanding, they will have their eyes on how they will eventually need to demonstrate what they are learning. The tenets of Understanding by Design present the structure to achieve this clarity and support.

Following these suggestions will allow you to enter and move through the inquiry pool with confidence. After you are comfortable with the first three Types of Student Inquiry, you'll be ready to embrace the most powerful type—the culmination of our journey through the inquiry pool together—Free Inquiry. In the following chapter, we'll look at the framework I have adopted for Free Inquiry, a few working models, and some specific components I have developed to best meet the needs of my students.

6

A Closer Look at Free Inquiry

Our entire course is scaffolded for the Free Inquiry unit. Students have been reflecting on essential questions, learning evidence, conducting research, and Understanding by Design throughout the year. By the time we get to our Free Inquiry unit, students are well prepared for the challenges they will face.

In this last unit of study, students experience a level of scaffolding similar to what they experienced throughout the other Types of Student Inquiry. So, while this type of inquiry is "Free," I firmly believe the increased level of voice and choice students are given requires a greater amount of structure and support. Therefore, our Free Inquiry unit is frontloaded with planning and attention to detail whilst simultaneously providing opportunities to reflect, revise, and re-plan as the unit unfolds.

This journey begins with the Inquiry Process, a framework I designed and have used over the years to help all students succeed in their Free Inquiry unit. This framework enables us to stay on track, reflect and revise as needed, and create a common structure we can all learn under despite the incredible amount of voice, choice, and personalisation we will achieve. Using the tenets of Understanding by Design, I created this framework where we plan with the end in mind, scaffold with rich and abundant opportunities to create understanding, and document and capture our learning as it happens.

There are seven steps in our Inquiry Process:
1. The Four Pillars of Inquiry
2. Creating an Essential Question
3. Create Your Free Inquiry Proposal
4. Begin to Explore and Research
5. Collect Learning Evidence
6. Create Your Authentic Piece
7. Public Display of Understanding

Each step scaffolds to the next, culminating in a public display of student understanding. Let's begin by looking at The Four Pillars of Inquiry.

7

The Four Pillars of Inquiry

I encourage students to spend time developing and completing an inquiry in each of the Four Pillars of Inquiry. My *dream* educational model would have students experience inquiry from kindergarten through twelfth grade. Thinking of the possibilities for students if they learned through an IBL model before they reach high school excites me. I am confident that if we gave students, from a young age, the opportunity to ask questions they were encouraged to explore, it would guide them to a more meaningful and enriched educational experience.

Over the years I have witnessed amazing things from students who structured their inquiry from one of these pillars.

Students are inclined to stick with their inquiry when the going gets tough.

Because their inquiry is rooted in one of the Four Pillars, students dig further into their research, stay up later at night exploring their driving question, and work harder when it comes time to demonstrate their understanding. Students don't procrastinate during their inquiry projects because they are so interested in answering their essential question and learning more about their area of interest. By empowering students in the direction of their education, we are nurturing an intrinsic motivation with awesome benefits.

> By empowering students in the direction of their education, we are nurturing an intrinsic motivation with awesome benefits.
>
> #DiveintoInquiry

Students' performance tasks are always more meaningful and personally fulfilling when rooted in one of the Four Pillars.

Because the passions they possess, the questions they ask, and the goals they set are all intensely meaningful to each student, genuine excitement about their question is evident in all aspects of their inquiry and performance task. Additionally, demonstrations of student learning are more compelling, speaking to the audience in a highly interesting and thought-provoking manner. Further, student's performance tasks are done to a higher standard because their passion and excitement for their topic consequently results in what we both perceive to be their best effort.

I am better able to meet the needs of all the students with whom I collaborate.

Some students are passionate about a particular topic, while others are not. Some students have burning questions and curiosities, while others do not. Some students are intensely goal focused, while others are not. And some students enjoy new challenges, while others do not. The Four Pillars empower students to embrace a certain level of personalisation in their inquiry and allow me to better support them throughout the year.

So what are the Four Pillars, and how can we begin to foster inquiry from them? Let's take a closer look.

EXPLORE A PASSION

Have you ever discovered—too late in the year—that a student in your class is immensely talented in a particular area? I can recall many such occasions from early in my career. I remember sitting in the audience at a school theatre production of *The Addams Family* and thinking, *Is that really Liam in the lead role? Quiet and shy Liam from my English class?* Or another time at a Christmas music recital when I realised Nicole, who always sat in the back row of class, was an extremely gifted violinist. Or at halftime of a varsity basketball game, when I watched Oliver lead the school dance troop in a breakdance performance. Or when I learned Julia was passionately involved in *Women without Borders* as she proposed a fundraising campaign at a staff meeting. And the list goes on and on.

These experiences remind me of two things: First, students are pretty amazing. They are talented, dedicated, curious, and passionate about what they decide to set their minds to. And second, their talents and passions—things they have fostered and honed outside of my relationship with them—are often unseen in class. I am always amazed that these students have been sitting right before me all year, and I had absolutely no idea they were so talented.

Students spend countless hours outside of class doing what they love. Some are committed to sports and the pursuit of athletic excellence. Day after day they practice, train, compete, and slowly become better and better at what they love. For some, their passion is reflected in the arts—dance, theatre, music, or the visual arts. I've seen students focus their inquiry on their love for auto-mechanics, video games, or metalwork. At times students' compassion for others drives their inquiry, illustrated in their involvement in social issues, environmental topics, or efforts against the discrimination and alienation of those less fortunate.

Beginning inquiry from a place of passion allows students to connect with something they've previously fostered and nurtured—and to which they've committed. They are excited when their passion is honoured in class! Furthermore, they're set up for success since they are beginning their inquiry plan with deeply meaningful and useful prior knowledge. Accessing this throughout the brainstorming stage aids the formation of their plan and their upcoming study.

> Beginning inquiry from a place of passion allows students to connect with something they've previously fostered and nurtured— and to which they've committed.
>
> #DiveintoInquiry

Zoe provides a great example. Her passion for figure skating led her through her Free Inquiry unit. You'll have no trouble seeing why she chose figure skating.

I am a figure skater and aspire to improve in my sport. My driving question is, What makes an elite athlete elite? As a growing athlete in such a refined sport, I was interested in discovering how I could improve. Factors such as confidence, goal setting, and nutrition contribute to an athlete becoming elite in her sport. Since I found these factors obvious, I wanted to go outside the norm and look into other components of success to help others and myself. Plus, this would be more interesting than simply researching and presenting the obvious to others. My passion for figure skating led me to develop my driving question. In researching it, I discovered new things I can do to improve.

To help answer her driving question, Zoe read *The Talent Code* by Daniel Coyle and applied what she learned from her research to her own figure skating practice. She then reflected on her progress over the course of several months and created this great, authentic piece to demonstrate what she learned about her essential question:

Some students, like Zoe, know exactly what their passions are. Others may need help exploring and identifying their passions. The following are some tools I use to get students to Explore a Passion:

PROVIDE PASSION PROMPTS

I use Passion Prompts to get students to reflect on what their passions may be. At times, I use prompts to get students writing thoughts about their passions. Other times, I write a prompt on the board and have students share their reflections in a group. Sometimes I pair students together and give each student a few prompts to use as they interview their partner. This method helps me gain valuable insight into what passions students may possess, and I can encourage and provide support as they dig deeper into topics leading to their Free Inquiry.

These are the Passion Prompts I use with my students:

- What are you passionate about?
- What are your talents?
- What motivates you?
- What do you naturally do well?
- What engages you?
- What excites you?
- What makes you feel awesome about yourself?
- What do you do in your free time?
- What would you do if you knew you could not fail?
- Whom do you look up to? Who are your mentors? Who inspires you? Why?
- Have you ever lost track of time doing something? What were you doing?
- Are you a member of a club or team? What is it? How long have you been a member?
- Have you ever spent a considerable amount of time learning something that wasn't for school? What was it?
- Are there any topics you find yourself consistently arguing or defending to others? What beliefs does your stance represent?
- Have you ever learned a new language? Did you learn this language for a trip or vacation to another country?
- In what ways do you love helping people?

- Do you play a musical instrument? How long did it take you to learn to play?
- What are some things you have accomplished in your life? What about these accomplishments are you most proud of?

SHOW A GENUINE PASSION FOR LEARNING

Have you ever felt someone else's passion so strongly it seemed to radiate off them? I love being around passionate people, and I always hear from my students how they love being around a passionate teacher. So I show my students videos—true stories documenting people's passions for a particular topic. By showing them passion in action, I believe students begin to grasp a potential starting place for their own passion and inquiry.

One of my favourite videos is *Caine's Arcade,* a short YouTube clip about a nine-year-old boy who, over his summer vacation at his father's auto parts shop, constructs the coolest cardboard game arcade you've ever seen. Caine represents the passion for learning I believe is in all students, especially at a younger age. Sadly, this passion slowly fades as students grow older and progress from grade to grade where curriculum is overemphasised, and standardised tests cause depersonalisation. By showing my students *Caine's Arcade,* I hope to reconnect them to the genuine passion for learning they felt before it got lost. I want them to feel excited about the opportunity to explore something they're passionate about through their inquiry.

Watch *Caine's Arcade* and ask yourself these questions I ask my students when they first view it:

- Why did Caine build his arcade?
- What do you think Caine's teachers would think of his arcade?
- If Caine was assigned to "build an arcade" at school, in what class do you think it would be assigned? Why?

- What do you think Caine learned in school that helped him build his arcade?
- How skilled is Caine at building cardboard arcade games?
- Where did he learn the skills needed to build all of his games?
- Was Caine's arcade a success? Why or why not?
- Do you think getting more customers makes his arcade more of a success? Why or why not?
- Do you think the social media momentum and flash mob makes his arcade more of a success? Why or why not?
- Do you think we could build something like Caine's arcade at our school? For which class would we build it?

Do you see Caine's arcade working in your classroom? Do you think your students would enjoy seeing Caine's passion on display?

Before we continue on to the other Pillars of Inquiry, I must share I have come to realise structuring my classroom and sculpting the curriculum around student passions can be tricky for two particular reasons: First, post-secondary institutions have pretty specific expectations impacting what is taught in certain high school courses; therefore, to some extent, provincial and state educational governing bodies design curriculum around these ends. Reconfiguring curriculum to focus solely on inquiry and student passions can become an uneven balance, where critical course content could be missed and leave lasting implications on a student's educational pathway. All courses contain a certain amount of must-know information, and there's no escaping that.

Second, passions are great, but you don't really know something is a passion until you bump into it, grapple with it, and after some time, find it interesting and worthy of your commitment. My current passions didn't start with my recognising them as such. For example, my love of cooking didn't start because I tinkered with recipes and ingredients thinking, *Oh my! I absolutely love cooking even though I have never done it before. I want to cook as much as I can because I absolutely love it!* At some point, I discovered I was interested in cooking and eventually I came to love it. Student passions are the same. Exploration, discovery, and time are all involved in a passion becoming a passion!

> Passions are great, but you don't really know something is a passion until you bump into it, grapple with it, and after some time, find it interesting and worthy of your commitment.
>
> #DiveintoInquiry

The other Pillars of Inquiry—Aim for a Goal, Delve into Your Curiosities, and Take On a New Challenge—provide a springboard for students to access valuable prior knowledge, begin from a place of a genuine intrinsic motivation, bump into a passion, and discover new and interesting possibilities they may not have considered before.

AIM FOR A GOAL

How is this relevant to my life? I used to struggle to find an answer when students asked me this question. I'd try to make connections to the importance of literacy, the benefit of studying and discussing rich literature, and the need to succeed on their year-end exams in order to get into a good university and get a good job; however, since I've adopted an inquiry model and our entire course is built on personalising learning, I don't hear this question anymore.

I love when students come into the classroom already knowing where they want to be in the future, having a strong career path in mind. I've worked with dozens of these students, and the second Pillar of Inquiry honours them by allowing them to explore more deeply where they want to be in their future and how they can get there.

Alicia is a great example. As she reflects below, her goal to become a registered nurse led her through her Free Inquiry unit.

> *Nursing is a fascinating career. My grandmother and mother were both nurses, and I aspire to be a nurse. Nurses take care of multiple lives, all fully dependent on the care and expertise of the nurse. The job exposes you to illness, disease, and unexpected challenges on a daily basis, but I find the opportunity to support the health and well-being of every patient is compelling. Because many skills are crucial to performing a nurse's daily task, and nursing is a stressful career, it is best for me to learn as much as I can before embarking on the long journey to become a registered nurse. Through reading A Nurse's Story by Tilda Shalof, interviewing my grandmother (who was a nurse from the late 1970s to late 1990s), and job-shadowing a clinical nurse at a local hospital, I will identify the skills of the average nurse and determine whether or not this is the career for me.*

To help Alicia answer her essential question, she interviewed her grandmother, read and researched an autobiography of a nurse, and visited a local hospital to witness first-hand what nurses do. Her goal of becoming a registered nurse guided her through her inquiry, led her to her resources, and inevitably provided her with rich and meaningful information about her future career goals.

Currently, two years removed from her Free Inquiry project, Alicia is preparing for convocation after completing her licensed practical nursing program. She has accepted a position that she will begin after graduation.

CONDUCT AN INTERVIEW

To help students identify a goal, I conduct an interview with them. I love asking them a few questions to get to know them better. I ask a bit about their future, where they see themselves in the next few years, and any work experience they have. My hope is to pinpoint a particular

> Through an interview we identify an inquiry topic that will help them gain valuable knowledge, work experience, and perhaps even post-secondary credit for their future plans.
>
> #DiveintoInquiry

area around which they could build an inquiry to help them gain valuable knowledge, work experience, and perhaps even post-secondary credit for their future plans. Some of the interview questions I ask are as follows:

- Are you certain about what you will do after you graduate? What will it be? Describe.
- Where do you want to be in five, ten, and twenty years?
- What steps should you be taking now to ensure the future you see for yourself becomes a reality?
- Is there a specific program or university to which you will apply? What first year courses do you plan to take?
- Is there an internship or work experience you would like to complete as part of your inquiry?
- If you could make a living doing what you love, what would it be?

- A MOOC is a Massive Open Online Course. Typically free and administered by a university professor, they encourage non-enrolled students to participate to broaden the learning community and enrich the learning experience. Is there a MOOC you can complete in preparation for your future career goals?
- Make a list of all the jobs you could see yourself doing. List what excites you—and what you anticipate you'd dislike—about each of these jobs.

I've co-constructed some amazing Free Inquiry units based on students' responses to these interviews. I learn so much about where they want to be and whether or not they have a plan to get there. I'm also able to connect them with resources necessary to get them on their way to achieving their future goals. We collaborate with career counsellors at our school, college, university, or volunteer organisations, hopefully to arrange a job experience placement. Together we map out particular steps to make the most of the Free Inquiry unit—and immediately get students started on their futures.

My experience with Eli exemplifies why conducting student interviews is so important. As a child, Eli was dragged to his older brother's baseball games, but instead of watching the action on the field, he was completely drawn to the paramedic crew onsite in case of injury or emergency. Eli asked questions, checked out the ambulance, and watched in fascination as the medical crew did their jobs.

By the age of nine, Eli had spent so much time at the first aid station, the crew made him a "junior paramedic," gave him a crew cap and badge, and asked him to do small jobs to support them. By the age of thirteen, Eli was volunteering his time to support the crew and became more involved with their responsibilities. And by the age of sixteen, Eli had completed his first-aid certification, was a licensed Emergency Medical Assistant, and was getting paid to be on the crew. Eli's dream was to become a paramedic and save lives, and clearly, he was well on his way to making this happen.

Before Eli sat down with me for an interview, I had no knowledge of any of this. To me, he seemed quiet, shy, and even lacking in confidence. As the interview unfolded, I began to see an awesome opportunity for Eli to access all the valuable knowledge and experience he had gained over the years. Eli's Free Inquiry unit included mapping out the process of applying to the paramedicine program of his choosing and getting his application package together. Further, Eli brought his crew's ambulance to school and gave our class the same tour he would give to people visiting him at events such as baseball tournaments. Isn't that amazing?

When reflecting on his Free Inquiry project, Eli stated the following:

I've been interested in paramedicine for as long as I can remember. Currently, I am a Non-Emergency Transport Medic at Medi-Van Canada where I drive ambulances and wheelchair-accessible buses. Primarily, I attend to patients in the back of the ambulances by checking vital signs and ensuring they are comfortable. In the future, I want to obtain my Primary Care Paramedic (PCP) license from the Justice Institute of British Columbia (JIBC) and work at the British Columbia Ambulance Service (BCAS). These are the same goals I have had since I was a young child.

As part of my inquiry project, I gave a presentation to my English class about one of the ambulances I work in. I let the students explore the ambulance on their own and then took groups of five or six students at a time into the back of the ambulance and gave an in-depth tour and answered their questions. Afterward, I attached my teacher, Mr. MacKenzie, to a spine board and ran through a quick scenario of what a paramedic would do on the scene of a real trauma call. I think this was the most valuable part of the presentation because everyone was exposed to paramedicine and seemed to enjoy watching it. And this presentation was the most enjoyable and rewarding project I have ever done in my school career.

Before this project, I was usually quite anxious about presenting anything—especially something personal—to my peers and usually became very quiet. But while presenting this project, I was more comfortable than I have ever been and was able to project my voice loudly. I had no problem answering questions even when asked in front of the large group. I feel the reason I did so well was because I was in one of the happiest and most comfortable places I know, and my comfort was one of the reasons the project was a success.

During this project, I experienced both personal and academic growth. I now feel more comfortable with my peers when I am in class. When I feel more comfortable, I am more emotionally present and, therefore, better equipped to learn. I think I will always remember and be proud of this project. Doing a presentation like this at school was a new experience for me—I'd never before had the opportunity to share with my peers something I am passionate about.

To help answer his essential question, Eli interviewed some of his colleagues who had graduated from the exact program he wanted to attend. He also researched the program online, toured the campus, and met with an academic advisor to map the application process. His goal to become a licensed paramedic guided him through his inquiry, led him to his resources, and inevitably provided him with rich and meaningful information about his future career goals.

This past year Eli put his application on hold and accepted a too-good-to-refuse job offer—working for a large-scale life support company that handles patient transfers via ambulance, helicopter, and plane. Eli travels internationally providing critical care for patients needing to return home. He has combined his career goal of becoming a licensed paramedic with his desire to travel and see the world. He plans on gaining a few years of valuable experience in this position before he applies to become a licensed paramedic.

DELVE INTO YOUR CURIOSITIES

Our third Pillar of Inquiry further strengthens the role of the student in shaping his journey through his educational experience. I'd estimate, prior to taking my course and experiencing inquiry in our classroom, students had questions given to them by their teachers throughout ninety percent of their schooling. For a variety of reasons, teachers select the topics, resources, and exam materials for their classes, and students have little to no voice in the process. If a student is quite interested in a specific area of a course, sadly there's a good chance she won't be able to really sink her teeth into it during school. So what does this student do when she has a burning question she'd love to answer but isn't provided the time, space, resources, or support to do it?

This is where the third Pillar of Inquiry, Delve into Your Curiosities, comes into play. Delving into your curiosities allows students to explore topics they've always wondered about but never had a chance to tackle. Topics could be offshoots of a passion or something they may have learned previously but would now like to investigate more deeply.

Delving into your curiosities allows students to explore topics they've always wondered about but never had a chance to tackle.

#DiveintoInquiry

I've used the following tools to help my students tap into their curiosities:

Create a Curiosity Journal.

Students can record their thoughts, wonders, and *what if* questions throughout the school year. The journal helps students begin the planning phase of their inquiry by getting them to think about and journal some questions they've been pondering. I suggest students begin a Curiosity Journal at the start of the year, asking them to record what they wonder about, what they're curious about, and what they've always wanted to know. This helps them create a log of possible inquiry projects on which they can reflect later.

I love asking students a few *what if* questions to see what's on their minds or what they are curious about. I often rely on five-minute free writes to get students to put their thoughts on paper. I'll prompt them with a thought-provoking question or statement and ask them to write down whatever comes to mind. My only request is they write for the entire five minutes. These are some prompts I've used:

- Have you ever taken something apart and tried to put it back together again? Share what it was and what you experienced. Were you successful? Did you discover anything new?
- What is the one thing you'd most like to change about the world?
- If happiness were the national currency, what kind of work would make you rich?
- If the average human lifespan were forty years, how would you live your life differently?
- If you could offer a newborn child only one piece of advice, what would it be?
- What one thing do you really want to do but haven't done yet? What's holding you back?

- If you had to move to a different country, where would you move, and why?
- At what time in your recent past have you felt most alive?
- What superpower would you choose to have for one day?
- What "most likely to" superlative accolade would you be most honoured to receive?
- If you could go back in time, what is one piece of advice you would give your younger self?
- What one experience would you be most disappointed to never have?
- If you could have been a child prodigy, what skill would you have wanted?
- What's the first thing you would do if you won the lottery?

If you could go back in time, what is one piece of advice you would give your younger self?

#DiveintoInquiry

What if questions lead to amazing learning opportunities. When educators structure lessons, unit plans, and assessments on top of student questions, the result is not only a more personalised learning pathway for the individual student, but also an open door for deeply meaningful and authentic learning experiences to occur.

Show Curiosity in Action.

I absolutely love showing my students real-life examples of curiosity. Whether in short YouTube clips, TEDx videos, documentaries, short stories, poems, nonfiction writings, or looking at student learning from previous classes, these examples show students where their curiosity can take them. Through these examples, students make connections and form excitement for their inquiry.

One example I love showing is a great video of a student whose curiosity led him on a three-year project. Matt Perren created a lip-sync animation to Queen's *Don't Stop Me Now,* demonstrating incredible attention to detail and technological proficiency. The end result was a time-lapse photo journey of his adolescence. Check it out here:

Another great video I enjoy sharing is about a young student from Sierra Leone, Kelvin Doe. Kelvin's love for inventing led him to create some unbelievable items from materials he scavenged from landfills and trash cans in his hometown. Local officials only turn on the electricity once a week, so Kelvin decided to try to build a homemade battery to help residents in his hometown power items when the electricity is off. Kelvin truly *learns* when he creates, and his genuine sense of curiosity has given him some fantastic opportunities. Have a watch here:

These videos are excellent examples of what students accomplish without prompting or teaching. Matt and Kelvin have spent countless hours developing specific skills they've used to help them tackle extremely challenging tasks, all of which was done outside of the classroom.

After viewing these videos together in class, we have small-group discussions leading into a larger class discussion. I ask my students the following questions:

- What motivated Matt and Kelvin to create what they did?
- What outcome have their creations had on them or others?
- When Matt and Kelvin first started their projects, do you think they set out to obtain the outcomes you've identified? Why or why not?
- What resonates with you most after watching these two videos? Why?
- Take five minutes to find a personal example illustrating how your own curiosity can lead to the creation of something unique, inspiring, or meaningful. Be prepared to share with others.

Ethan T. was a student of mine whose deep curiosity to discover the definition of happiness led him through his Free Inquiry unit. His reflections are compelling:

> *What is the definition of happiness? was my essential question for my IBL project in my English class this semester. While this seems like a broad and difficult question to answer, I love it because it's open to so much interpretation and has an infinite number of answers. I have always been curious why western society tends to feel less happy than other cultures of the world. I believe what we think is happiness is actually just a pleasure. Therefore, I think it's important we know the difference between happiness and pleasure and try to find what makes us actually happy.*

To answer his essential question, Ethan read Mark Kingwell's *In Pursuit of Happiness*, interviewed a psychology professor at a local university, and interviewed his friends and classmates. He combined his love for videography and digital editing with his understanding of his essential question to create this superb authentic piece:

Aidan was another student who became increasingly curious about how to better meet the learning needs of gifted students. Aidan introduced his Free Inquiry unit and described why he chose to delve into the topic of gifted education:

> I chose gifted education for my Inquiry-Based Learning project after my English 12 class was paired up with a second-grade class at a local elementary school for a buddy reading project. My little buddy was a young boy named Rowan, whom I immediately noticed was a proficient reader, far ahead of the rest of his classmates. After our first session, his teacher explained to me that Rowan read at an eighth-grade level, six years ahead of the rest of his class.
>
> As we continued to meet with the second graders, it became apparent to me Rowan learned differently than other students in his class, reading novels whilst his peers read introductory-reading books. Rowan's reading level was years ahead of his age, but he still had to learn at the level administrators had determined for him.
>
> I started wondering, What if Rowan could be in a higher learning environment? What if he could learn with other students who were at his level of intellect? How would he respond to the accelerated content?
>
> So I took advantage of my Free Inquiry project for my English 12 course and studied this essential question: How can we better accommodate gifted minds in today's education system?
>
> I decided my authentic piece of the project would be bringing Rowan to my high school and have him sit in on several

eleventh- and twelfth-grade courses. I wanted to see how he would react and respond to the course content to determine if he would enjoy being in a higher level of education. I also hoped this field trip would get Rowan excited about what his future as a learner could look like.

In answering his essential question, Aidan read several essays, articles, and interviews calling for a transformation to our educational system. He also collaborated with Rowan's parents, asking Rowan's mother to join him for his visit to our school. Underlying his entire Free Inquiry unit was Aidan's desire to get Rowan excited about learning. During their weekly reading sessions, Aidan worked on accelerated activities with Rowan and tried to personalise this time as much as he could to suit Rowan's gifted characteristics, making it a highly meaningful experience for everyone involved.

TAKE ON A NEW CHALLENGE

The fourth Pillar of Inquiry, Take On a New Challenge, builds on the previous three pillars and provides one last layer for empowering students in our classroom. Taking on a New Challenge calls on students to consider focusing their inquiry in an area of personal endeavour.

Students can tackle something they've wanted to dive into. The challenge could be anything from learning a new language or musical instrument to confronting a social issue such as local poverty, or a school issue such as connectedness. They could even explore a broader, more global challenge such as inequality in a developing nation. Whatever they choose, the fourth Pillar of Inquiry provides the foundation for student inquiry to be personally meaningful and engaging.

To inspire students to Take On a New Challenge, I utilise several activities:

Introduce Frequent Small-Group Challenges.

I spend a little bit of time each term introducing my classes to something I think most of them have little experience with. I love bringing my passion for innovation and technology into our classroom. At times, I have introduced my students to coding via Scratch or The Hour of Code. Both are great, free online visual programming websites allowing students to easily grasp and practice coding skills. At other times, I have created a Makerspace challenge collaborating with our woodworking teacher. Together, we pitch a small scale design and execute a group project. Students especially enjoy when I bring our *Lego Mindstorm* robotic kits from our computer technology course into our classroom. With these, I challenge my students to design and program a robot in small groups. I also love using the 3-D printer at our school to show students some basic modelling, printing, and finishing skills.

In all of these cases, I possess a good skill set and feel pretty comfortable guiding them through the various challenges whilst scaffolding our inquiry and guiding them to consider challenges of their own.

Another great activity we do is Breakout EDU. Breakout EDU is an exciting classroom game that fosters critical thinking, collaboration, and creativity. Players are presented with some sort of a collective challenge and a locked box. The solution to the challenge resides inside the box; however, in order to unlock the box and complete the game, students must use a series of clues to solve several mystery challenges over a given amount of time. The group's ability to successfully navigate these challenges determines if they complete the game.

My kids love Breakout EDU. The challenge I pitch, the clues they face, and the time running out all lend to an engaging and suspenseful activity. Plus, I love seeing them work together to figure out how to best succeed in their quest to open the box. They repeatedly bump against roadblocks and obstacles that would make many of them struggle and give up if they were facing them alone. But when facing these challenges in a group, they support one another and leave no teammate behind. Inspiring to witness, Breakout EDU is fun for the class and fosters many of the soft skills I love to nurture in my room.

Introduce a Single Long-Term Group Challenge.

I have found students want to have a genuine impact on others. They want their time at school to have a real-world impact, either with their learning connecting to the world around them or by their actions having meaning and power. If we can help bridge this divide between "school" and "life," amazing things begin to happen. So I challenge them to make a difference in other people's lives.

> Students want to have a genuine impact on others, and if we can bridge the divide between school and life, amazing things will happen.
>
> #DiveintoInquiry

One vehicle for this in our classroom is a literacy project in collaboration with our local elementary school. For about two months, my students visit a first- through fifth-grade class each week to write a children's book. We spend the initial weeks getting to know as many of the "buddies" as we can. We read to or with a few of them each visit, and eventually each student partners with a specific student with whom to spend the remainder of the project.

We brainstorm a story, begin to draft a narrative, draw the illustrations, and towards the end of the project, put the finishing touches on the published piece. We close out the project by inviting our buddy class to our school on a field trip. We escort them to our school, give them a short tour, and give them our storybooks as a parting gift.

The impact on all the students is inspiring. The connections are meaningful and genuine. The older buddies thoughtfully chose their younger buddies because they identified with them or they saw a bit of themselves in the younger students. And the younger buddies look forward to our weekly visits with great anticipation. They talk and write about our partnership throughout the week. And further, the one-on-one reading time provides the younger students with a bit of focused and nurtured support, inevitably leading to improved literacy.

Ethan N. is a great example of a student who used the fourth Pillar of Inquiry to inspire his Free Inquiry. Ethan loved auto mechanics, but he faced a huge challenge when attempting to rebuild his Bazoo and decided to take on this new challenge for his Free Inquiry project.

> *In English 12, we were faced with an Inquiry-Based Learning project where we had to find an essential question that challenged us. I love auto mechanics—working on and fixing up anything with a motor. This past summer I bought a Bazoo, an amphibious vehicle built in the 1970s. I got it off of Craigslist, and it lead me to my essential question: Has mechanical technology significantly changed in the past forty years? Can I rebuild my Bazoo? I chose this question because I am quite interested in mechanical technology, and there is no repair manual for my Bazoo. Taking on the task of rebuilding this machine with modern tools and parts in order to answer the question would be a huge challenge, but I was up for it!*

To answer his essential question, Ethan used several manuals and texts from his auto courses at our school. Further, he watched dozens of YouTube videos and received valuable information when he posted and discussed problems he encountered on forums focused on auto repair.

Ethan N.'s Free Inquiry unit was eye-opening to me in a couple of ways: First, when Ethan was struggling to find helpful information during his research, he went directly to the professionals in the field. By posting questions to auto forums and communicating with mechanics across the world, he not only got the answers he was looking for, but also demonstrated that there is not just one clear-cut route to answering essential questions. What Ethan needed to answer his essential question was different from what others in our class needed. He faced an authentic challenge in his research, was mindful, critical, and creative in how he handled this challenge, and demonstrated that not all the answers are in the back of the book. I most certainly wouldn't have been able to suggest this research path.

> There is not just one clear-cut route to answering essential questions.
>
> #DiveintoInquiry

Second, Ethan's project led me to make a decisive shift about how I could best support students in their learning. One day, whilst I was conducting check-ins with students and reviewing their learning evidence, I glanced up and saw Ethan, sitting at his desk, bored out of his mind. I was shocked. Over the course of rebuilding his Bazoo, Ethan had been excited, engaged, and loving this Free Inquiry unit. Not on this particular day, though, and I was baffled. When I asked him why, his answer was so plain, simple, and obvious, I was embarrassed I hadn't seen it coming.

All of Ethan's work was at home. And for once in my career, I understood the magnitude of this "excuse" I had received countless times before. His garage, his shop, his tools, his Bazoo—everything he needed to further his learning and answer his essential question—was at home, not at school.

So Ethan and I hatched a plan to give him the space to be connected to his learning and provide me the evidence I was hoping to see. We agreed Ethan wouldn't attend class for several weeks of his Free Inquiry unit; rather, he'd work on his Bazoo from home and email me video footage of his progress each day in the form of a time-lapse photo journal so I could see how he was spending his time away from class. Ethan's *home*work comprised over sixty hours of work.

How exciting! I've always believed learning isn't confined to our school bell schedule and the brief time I work with students each day. But I've also believed homework, in most cases, is pretty pointless. But Ethan's time-lapses demonstrated that meaningful and authentic learning outside of school can be brought into and honoured in our classrooms.

> # Meaningful and authentic learning outside of school can be brought into and honoured in our classroom.
>
> #DiveintoInquiry

Did Ethan succeed in rebuilding his Bazoo? His plan was to bring his fully operational Bazoo to school on a flatbed trailer and present it to our class on our soccer field. Take a look at Ethan's concluding video:

Things were coming to an end in our semester. Authentic pieces were being shared, students were reflecting on their learning, and Ethan came to discuss with me his final grade in the course. He was concerned that since he hadn't succeeded in rebuilding his Bazoo, he would fail the unit. Ethan couldn't have been more wrong. I asked Ethan to reflect on how much he had learned in answering his essential question, how much progress he had made on his Bazoo, and whether or not this process was meaningful to him.

We realized Ethan's project utilised three important elements:

- a strongly scaffolded unit plan using the tenets of Understanding by Design
- plenty of opportunity for support, reflection, and revision
- a performance task focused on reflection rather than on success in answering his essential question

The combination of these helped Ethan and me to collaboratively assess his unit in a clear, precise, and accurate manner. Although his Bazoo wasn't fully operational, we agreed his Free Inquiry unit was a resounding success.

Now for the coolest part: Over a year after our course and his graduation, Ethan reached out to me to share that he had completed his Bazoo. He has recently taken it out for its maiden voyage and sent me this clip:

Look at the family members recording the event. Look at the mix of uncertainty and excitement on the faces of everyone involved. Look at Ethan driving his Bazoo. Now imagine the pride and sense of accomplishment he must feel. Without adopting an inquiry model, the authentic and lifelong learning evident in this video would not be possible in my classroom.

Have you ever had a student hand
in homework a year late? I have,
and it taught me that learning
doesn't have a due date.

#DiveintoInquiry

8

Essential Questions

After I introduce students to the Four Pillars of Inquiry, they choose an inquiry topic they'd like to focus on for their Free Inquiry unit. Our challenge now becomes turning this inquiry topic into an essential question. Since we have been using essential questions throughout the year, by the time we get to our Free Inquiry unit, students have a strong grasp on what they are, what they provide, and how to write them. But this process of going from an inquiry topic to gaining broader understanding of the topic to drafting an essential question merits a closer look.

Before they draft essential questions, students have time and space to dig into their inquiry topic. I ask them to conduct preliminary brainstorming and research. We determine what they already know about their topic—known as activating prior knowledge—and begin with the always reliable *who, what, where, when, why,* and *how* questions. From the answers to these, students gain a broad stroke of understanding which provides context and background for their inquiry topic.

We then move on to unpack resources from our library and online. Exploring the inquiry topic and wading through strong resources before students hash out their essential question is a valuable part of the essential question process. In my experience, when students are given an abundance of resources with which to browse, skim, and interact, they form a clearer direction for their inquiry and a stronger essential question.

When students are given an abundance of resources with which to browse, skim, and interact, they form a clearer direction for their inquiry and a stronger essential question.

#DiveintoInquiry

In my classroom, we collaborate with our school librarian. After surveying students and compiling a list of their potential inquiry topics, our librarian and I pull resources, do a bit of digging into the online databases to which we have access, and look for any other relevant sources of information we can provide. My class then visits the library, and the librarian and I walk the class through a couple of things:

We first show them the resources we located for their specific inquiry topics. We aim to have three resources for each student to ensure they all have a few items to explore. The resources are laid out across tables, and students are encouraged to check out titles, read the synopses on the backs of the books, and skim a few pages looking for immediate relevance to their inquiry topic. We then show students our online databases and introduce them to important tips for searching them. We ask that they retrieve relevant information to help them form a direction for their essential question. Our goal during this time is to give students a few resources on their inquiry topic to provide a foundation for their more specific essential question.

CHARACTERISTICS OF ESSENTIAL QUESTIONS

Once students have had time to dig into their inquiry topic and unpack a few resources, our attention turns to transforming this topic into an essential question to guide learning. Two resources in particular have strengthened my own understanding of this process and provided me with the tools I use to support my students to become strong creators of essential questions: *Essential Questions: Opening Doors to Student Understanding* by Jay McTighe and Grant Wiggins, and *Make Just One Change: Teach Students to Ask Their Own Questions* by Dan Rothstein and Luz Santana. These books provide context, connections, and examples I have found invaluable to transforming my classroom into an inquiry-based learning community. From them, I have gleaned characteristics of essential questions I teach my students to use as they draft their own. The Question Formulation Technique (QFT) is one specific tool I have implemented in my practice that I have found invaluable. *Make Just One Change* outlines the QFT teaching strategy which provides a simple, yet powerful, way to ask their own questions. I strongly encourage you to seek out both of these resources as you dive further into inquiry.

A strong essential question must be open-ended.

Essential questions are not answered in a quick, simple Google search. They are not answered in a single lesson or in a discussion with a friend. They do not have a single answer and, in fact, our understanding of the essential question may change over time. Essential questions require higher-order thinking such as analysis, inference, evaluation, and prediction. Over time, they may raise additional questions and inspire further inquiry.

A strong essential question must provide the depth of study demanded by our course.

An essential question in a junior level science class will look quite different from an essential question in a senior level chemistry class. The course and grade level will shape how thought-provoking and intellectually engaging each essential question must be, and our student's demonstration of understanding will require a level of support and justification determined by the course and grade level.

A strong essential question must be meaningful to the student.

Although the Four Pillars of Inquiry are designed to lead the students to meaningful questions, I still ask each student, "How is your question meaningful to you?" The responses are always rich and personal. At the conclusion of the unit, when the students publicly share their work, I encourage them to include why their essential question is meaningful to them. Their reflections hook the audience and create a shared excitement for their inquiry.

Students have to think critically to answer an essential question. Instead of simply looking up answers, they conduct research and create an original answer. In addition to the characteristics above, the following characteristics are posted in our classroom to remind students

> Students have to think critically to answer an essential question. Instead of simply looking up answers, they conduct research and create an original answer.
>
> #DiveintoInquiry

what their essential question should achieve. An essential question should...

- provoke deep thought
- solicit information-gathering and evaluation of data
- result in an original answer
- help students conduct problem-related research
- make students produce original ideas rather than predetermined answers
- encourage critical thinking, not just memorisation of facts

Lastly, an essential question may not have an answer.

GETTING STUDENTS STARTED

To help students begin drafting essential questions, I suggest they start with the following:

- Which one?
- How?
- What if?
- Should?
- Why?

Which one questions call for students to weigh two options and provide evidence supporting one over the other. *How* questions ask students to evaluate, infer, and perhaps propose alternatives. *What if* questions are hypothetical and ask students to use the knowledge they already have to pose a hypothesis and consider options. *Should* questions request a moral or practical decision based on evidence. *Why* questions ask students to understand cause and effect and help them understand relationships. They help students get to the essence of an issue.

I take these essential question stems further and provide the following list to the students to use as they draft their own essential questions:

- How would you … ?
- What would result if … ?
- How would you describe … ?
- How does…compare with … ?
- What is the relationship between … and … ?
- How could you change … ?
- How would you improve … ?
- How do you feel about … ?
- Why do you believe … ?
- What is your opinion of … ?
- What choice would you have made … ?
- What would you do differently … ?
- Why do you feel … ?
- How would you go about solving the problem … ?
- If you were in this position, would you … ?
- Why do you/don't you support … ?
- What could improve … ?

Each student drafts a few questions we can discuss together in a one-on-one meeting. My goal for these meetings is to ensure their essential questions meet the above characteristics. I ask each student these three questions:

- Is your essential question open-ended?
- Does your essential question provide the depth of study demanded by our course?
- How is your essential question meaningful to you?

During these meetings, I may suggest revisions to help students meet the above characteristics. I try to gain an understanding of what information brought them to the essential questions they've created. I often offer up resources to help guide their inquiry. And at times, I share essential questions and Free Inquiry projects from previous students to help direct or inspire students in their own inquiry. At the end of the meeting, each student has an essential question they can use to guide their Free Inquiry unit.

9

The Free Inquiry Proposal: the Plan and the Pitch

With their essential question in hand, students are ready to plan their Free Inquiry unit. We tackle this planning by creating a Free Inquiry Proposal.

Over the years I have pinpointed a number of items students need to plan from the onset of their Free Inquiry unit. These ensure students grasp the scope of their undertaking, identify the critical components needed to scaffold understanding, and use the tenets of Understanding by Design to plan their unit.

Free Inquiry Proposal

By:@trev.mackenzie

1. What is your essential question? Please share why it is meaningful to you.

2. What is your authentic piece? How will you make your learning public?

3. What will you read, research and study to help explore your essential question?

4. What are your goals for your free inquiry?

5. What learning evidence will you gather to capture everything you are learning about your essential question?

6. What is your plan? Create a calendar and day-to-day plan to help your free inquiry unit to be a successful learning experience.

The Free Inquiry Proposal is composed of six sections:

1. What is your essential question? Why is it meaningful to you?
2. What is your authentic piece? How will you make your learning public?
3. What will you read, research, and study to help explore your essential question?
4. What are your goals for your Free Inquiry?
5. What learning evidence will you gather to capture everything you are learning about your essential question?
6. What is your plan? Create a calendar and day-to-day plan to help your Free Inquiry unit to be a successful learning experience.

During this process, students plan and pitch their entire Free Inquiry unit to me. They identify a topic for their inquiry, possible information sources, an audience and presentation format, some evaluation criteria, and how they will retrieve and record information in the form of their learning evidence. Finally, they outline their plan for their inquiry.

THE PLAN

A closer look at each of these sections will equip us to best help students plan out their Free Inquiry unit.

Section 1: What is your essential question? Why is it meaningful to you?

Students build on the excellent work they did to draft their essential question. I ask them to state their essential question and describe how it is personally meaningful to them. This gives me a good sense of not only *why* they've selected their inquiry topic but also how they might hook their audience when it's time to share their learning. In fact, most students will revisit this section of their proposal and use their reflection as an introduction to their authentic piece because they feel it will

Sharing why learning is meaningful to each student is a powerful shift afforded by the inquiry model.

#DiveintoInquiry

help their audience understand the background of their inquiry and the drive behind their essential question. This question is rooted in the work we have done using the Four Pillars of Inquiry and which pillar the learner has founded their inquiry topic on. I ask students to touch down on this point as they share why their essential question is meaningful to them.

A great example of an essential question comes from Caden. His essential question and inquiry topic were deeply personal, and it was this connection between his life and his learning that guided his inquiry.

> My essential question is, how can nutrition impact disease?
>
> I chose this topic for my IBL project because it hit pretty close to home. Two years ago my father had a heart attack (Ventricular tachycardia) which affected the electrical system of his heart and he almost lost his life. He was then diagnosed with a progressive heart disease (Arrhythmogenic right ventricular cardiomyopathy) which was causing the electrical problem. We were told that he would be on medication for the rest of his life to control the attacks, not be able to exercise or stress his heart and would live like this for the rest of his days, no longer having a normal life. The doctor's said that it was a genetic condition and that there was nothing we could do.

As a family, we did not accept this prognosis, and that's when our research began. We discovered a huge amount of knowledge and information on self-healing through nutrition. Six months later, after a great deal of research about natural healing, my father made a decision against the cardiologist's advice on what therapy he wanted to follow. He strictly followed the chosen therapy and, within a month, he had slowly cycled himself off the medication. He immediately felt and experienced changes in his body. Once he was free of the medication the attacks completely stopped. He has not had another attack in a year and a half, is exercising regularly running about 5 km every second day, and has been following resistance training with weights without a single incident. He has continued with this program and his health continues to improve each day. My father is alive simply because of proper nutrition. He is a living example that not only do natural methods work but also that there isn't just one method of treatment for an illness. When you provide the body with proper nutrition, the whole body heals. This is why my essential question is meaningful to me.

Section 2: What is your authentic piece? How will you make your learning public?

Students design a large part of the performance task they will create to demonstrate their understanding of their essential question. To help them decide on a performance task, I ask them, "If you could demonstrate your understanding in any way, what would it be? Are you really good at something you feel would help communicate your understanding of your essential question?"

I strongly encourage students to include a digital element to their performance task. A digital authentic piece lives on, engages the audience, and allows students to share their learning publicly via blogs, websites, or social media.

Further, the work students produce should reflect the learning standards and expectations of the course. They can comment in their proposal how this is being done. Most will comment on the must-know portion of the curriculum and how their essential question and authentic piece relates to the demands of the course. This is an excellent way to further make the learning standards transparent and personally relevant to our students.

Section 3: What will you read, research, and study to help explore your essential question?

Students identify the preliminary strands of their research. These resources represent the foundational pieces students will unpack in order to explore their essential question. Undoubtedly, students will branch off from these sources of information as they learn more about their inquiry topic, become inspired in a particular direction, or ask new questions connected to their essential question. But before they do so, we need to ensure they have a strong starting point from which to begin their Free Inquiry unit.

Section 4: What are your goals for your Free Inquiry?

Students identify a few goals they have for their Free Inquiry unit. These goals could be academic and connected to a certain grade or mark in the course. But these goals could be something more abstract and challenging to assess. *Does my learning have an impact on the world around me? Does my authentic piece resonate with my audience? Have I created positive change in my community?* These are all examples of goals students have had in past Free Inquiry units. By asking students to share their goals for their inquiry, teachers can begin to better understand how to best support student inquiry and help students achieve their goals.

Section 5: What learning evidence will you gather to capture everything you are learning about your essential question?

Later in the book, I go into greater detail about learning evidence, but students essentially share how they will capture and document their learning as it happens. This will be a two-step process for students: The first is learning evidence, capturing the retrieval of information from student research. Note taking is a great example many students utilise. The second is learning evidence capturing the processing of information from student research. First-person journaling and questioning one's retrieval notes are great examples. Both of these methods should be outlined in this section of the proposal.

Section 6: What is your plan? Create a calendar and day-to-day plan to help your Free Inquiry unit to be a successful learning experience.

Students map out the big milestones of their Free Inquiry unit on a calendar template. Using what they've learned about Understanding by Design throughout the year, students first identify a date for their public display of learning and begin to work backwards from there. They map out what needs to be accomplished each week in order to stay on track and deal with any challenges they may face. Throughout the unit, we will revisit this plan and revise it where necessary. I tell students it is rare for a plan from the proposal stage not to be revised at some point in a Free Inquiry unit. Life can get in the way and research can take us in unforeseen directions, so the ability to revise throughout the inquiry process—to ensure success—is an immensely valuable skill.

> The ability to self-assess and revise throughout the inquiry process to ensure success is an immensely valuable skill.
>
> #DiveintoInquiry

Have a look at Katherine's original plan. She has done an exceptional job outlining various commitments outside of her inquiry project as well as several key dates by which she would like to have specific learning evidence completed. Her calendar allows her to see the end of her inquiry project and plan accordingly. I love how she included a catch-up day on May 11, where she states, "My plans are ambitious, so I may fall behind".

Step 6: Set up your timeline

SUNDAY	MONDAY	TUESDAY	WEDNESDAY	THURSDAY	FRIDAY	SATURDAY
April 20 Work 5:15am-12:06	**21**	**22**	**23**	**24** Work 4-7 pm	**25** Finish Dogwood Scholarship Portfolio annotations	**26** Finish draft of project proposal Spanish practice exam
27 Finish half of "Still Alice" Edit project proposal Work 5:15am-12	**28** Project Proposal Due	**29** Find one academic source for Alzheimer's research	**30** Read "Still Alice" Dogwood District Scholarship Due	**May 1** Read "Still Alice" Dogwood Community Scholarship Due Work 4-7 pm	**2** Finish "Still Alice"	**3** Brainstorm and outline of synthesis piece and final essay Blood Drive
4 Body of synthesis essay Work 5:15am-12	**5** Finish draft of synthesis essay	**6** Edit synthesis essay Journal #3	**7** Synthesis Piece Due	**8** Half of outline of personalized project	**9** Outline of personalized project	**10** 1/3 of draft of personalized project First round of editing on Essay
11 Catch-up Day (my plans are ambitious, so I may fall behind) Work 5:15am-12	**12** 2nd round of editing on Essay	**13** Catch-up Day (following the French AP Exam, I may fall behind) French AP Exam – will leave class early	**14** Journal #4 1/2 of draft of personalized project	**15** 3rd round of editing on Essay 2/3 of draft of personalized project Work 4-7 pm	**16** Finish draft of personalized project	**17** Finish essay 1st round of editing on personalized project
18 2nd round of editing on personalized project Work 5:15am-12	**19** Finalize personalized project	**20** Compile and package entire project in a due-tang or other suitable medium for submission; post written work on blog	**21** Project Due	**22** Work 4-7 pm	**23**	**24**

Now have a look at Katherine's revised plan. Notice how she has revised certain scheduled pieces of her inquiry and kept others. She kept her original due date for her project to be completed. I like to call on students to use their calendar each day and reflect on it each week. I ask them to make changes accordingly and, at the half-way point in our Free Inquiry unit, to submit a revised calendar to me for my records.

Step 6: Set up your timeline

Krause 6

SUNDAY	MONDAY	TUESDAY	WEDNESDAY	THURSDAY	FRIDAY	SATURDAY
April 20 — Work 5:15am-12:30	**21**	**22**	**23**	**24** — Work 4-7 pm	**25** — Finish Dogwood Scholarship Portfolio annotations	**26** — Finish draft of project proposal; Spanish practice exam
27 — Finish half of "Still Alice"; Edit project proposal; Work 5:15am-12	**28** — Project Proposal Due	**29** — Find one academic source for Alzheimer's research	**30** — Journal #2 Read "Still Alice"; Dogwood District Scholarship Due	**May 1** — Read "Still Alice"; Beacon Community Scholarship Due; Work 4-7 pm	**2** — Finish "Still Alice"	**3** — Brainstorm and outline of synthesis piece and final essay; Blood Drive
4 — Body of synthesis essay; Work 5:15am-14	**5** — Finish draft of synthesis essay	**6** — Edit synthesis essay; Journal #3; Spanish AP Exam – will not be in class; Physics Test! Blood Drive After school	**7** — Synthesis Piece Due; Blood Drive	**8** — Second body paragraph on Essay; Blood Drive; Work 4-7pm	**9** — Finish draft of Essay; Journal #3 Due; Physics Retest	**10** — Outline of Personalized Project; First round of editing on Essay; French practice exam
11 — Poem #1; Work 5:15am-12	**12** — 2nd round of editing on Essay; Poem #2	**13** — Poem #3 and #4; French AP Exam	**14** — Journal #4; 3rd round of editing on Essay; Chemistry competition	**15** — Poem #5; UVic appointment @ 11:15; Physics test? Work 4-7 pm	**16** — Finish Essay	**17** — Write introduction piece to poetry; 1st round of editing on personalized project
18 — 2nd round of editing on personalized project; Work 5:15am-9:30	**19** — Finalize personalized project	**20** — Compile and package entire project in a duo-tang or other suitable medium for submission; post written work on blog	**21** — Project Due	**22** — Work 4-7 pm	**23**	**24**

THE PITCH

After students have completed each section of their plan, we move to the second part of the Proposal: a one-on-one meeting where we discuss their plan and students pitch me on their Free Inquiry unit. I ask them to elaborate on their Proposal, and I review their plan to ensure their scope is manageable and achievable. Learning objectives of the course are included, learning evidence scaffolds their authentic piece and performance task, and the students are prepared to publicly display their work. I schedule these one-on-one meetings over the course of a few days and have students sign up for a timeslot that works for them. As I am meeting with one student, the rest of the class stays busy preparing for their own individual pitch. Students love completing mock pitches where they share their pitch with a peer to simulate what they will encounter when they meet with me. This allows for some extremely useful peer feedback and helps ensure the students have a strong pitch. At times I have scheduled one-on-one meet-

Peer feedback and self-assessment drive success.

#DiveintoInquiry

ings while the rest of the class participates in mock-pitch activities. However you decide to complete this process, be sure to honour each particular learner during the one-on-one pitch by giving them your full attention and asking them meaningful questions about their plan.

The scope should be manageable and achievable.

I look at their authentic piece and their calendar and evaluate whether or not the student has considered the demands of completing their plan and adequately planned for success. I look at their research plan and evaluate if the resources they've identified will provide them with the content to eventually deepen their understanding. Finally, I may make suggestions for change, ask questions for clarification, or praise students for what they've achieved.

A former student proposed writing a 150-page novella as her authentic piece for her Free Inquiry unit. During our proposal meeting, I reviewed her calendar to ensure she had allotted herself ample writing time to achieve the task and questioned her on a number of fronts:

- Have you written this much before?
- Do *you* think your goal is achievable?
- How motivated are you to complete your novella?
- Are you open to revising your plan part way through your inquiry if the challenge of completing the performance task becomes too great?
- Why is this authentic piece meaningful to you?

She explained that she aspired to be a writer and had plans to pursue creative writing the following year at university. I was confident this student would work her hardest to complete her novella.

The Free Inquiry unit must meet the learning objectives of the course.

As I review each student's plan, I look for evidence showing their Free Inquiry unit fits into the learning objectives of the course. At the start of the school year, we spent powerful time together co-creating our course outline. During this process, I outlined several must-know pieces we'd have to spend time unpacking, no matter what they wanted to study, read, discuss, or understand. I work hard to hit these learning standards throughout the Structured, Controlled, and Guided units leading to their Free Inquiry unit and ask students to build on these units and ensure the following:

- Their essential question meets or surpasses the intellectual rigor of the course.
- Their research, and whatever they are unpacking to help them deepen their understanding of their essential question, is at or above grade level.
- Their authentic piece reflects the learning standards of our course.

Identify how learners will show learning and demonstrate their learning and success in their inquiry.

- Regardless of how they plan to demonstrate understanding at the conclusion of the unit, their learning evidence must show they are preparing for this demonstration to be successful. As shared in chapter five, we define learning evidence in our classroom as any evidence of learning throughout their unit and deepening of their understanding of their essential question.
- Learning evidence in the form of note taking, summarising, questioning, or journaling can be pretty straightforward. Throughout the year, we discuss Learning evidence as we are doing it and identify how it scaffolds our performance task. In our Free Inquiry unit, learning evidence becomes unique and takes on highly personalised forms. Because authentic pieces open up the performance task to more options than our previous Structured, Controlled, and perhaps Guided Inquiry units, students must choose learning evidence to scaffold for their own specific authentic piece. To help students select appropriate learning evidence for their Free Inquiry unit, I provide some examples for a variety of authentic pieces I have seen students produce over the years.

Authentic Piece or Performances	Learning Evidence
Written (e.g., essay, short story, novella)	Brainstorms, notes, storyboard, drafts, edits (self, peer, and teacher edits)
Digital Recording (e.g., video)	Compilation of resources (what you will include in your video), takes, drafts, storyboard
Visual Art (e.g., paintings, graphic novels, illustrations)	Sketches, photos or time lapse of the work being created, the creation process, storyboard, opportunities for feedback and revision from someone with experience in this area (e.g., artist, graphic novelist)
Presentation (e.g., Prezi, PowerPoint, Keynote)	Compilation of resources (what you will include in your presentation), takes, drafts, storyboard
Photography	Brainstorms, plans, an abundance of attempts that lead to a narrowing of your published work, opportunities for feedback and revision from someone with experience in this area (i.e., professional photographer)
Dance	Brainstorms, plans, choreography, rehearsals, photos and video for self-reflection and assessment, collaboration with a dance teacher, instructor, or professional dancer
Drama Performance	Brainstorms, notes, storyboard, drafts, scripts, prop list, set design plan, edits (self, peer, and teacher edits), dress rehearsals, collaboration with a theatre teacher or director

Selecting their own learning evidence for their authentic piece—an exciting component of our Free Inquiry unit—empowers students to begin taking ownership over the assessment of their learning. They select documentation methods effective for their learning style, their performance task, and their needs. Highly metacognitive, this process is extremely empowering for all of us. Students get to self-assess throughout their learning, and I acquire a better understanding of what type of assessment works for each individual student.

Selecting learning evidence empowers students to begin taking ownership over the assessment of their learning.

#DiveintoInquiry

Their authentic piece, and a good portion of their learning, must be publicly displayed.

When students share their understanding beyond their classmates and me, amazing things happen. They are often celebrated by unforeseen admirers or supported by unanticipated professionals in their field. I am always pleasantly surprised with the connections born from this public display.

I am flexible and open to ideas about how this public display of learning may occur. In my English classes, all of my students create and maintain a blog as an e-portfolio of their learning throughout the year. These blogs are a great place for students to publish their learning. In other cases, I have co-planned events with students so they can share their learning with an authentic audience—a Science Fair, a gallery walk with other students, an Inquiry Open House where we invite friends, family, and mentors to view our learning, or any other opportunity where we can engage with an audience outside of our classroom.

Public displays of learning are a powerful tool in the classroom to further the connection between how student learning is meaningful and important to the world around them.

After the proposal discussion and helping students revise their plan (if necessary) to ensure their Free Inquiry unit is successful, I keep all the proposals alphabetised in an inquiry binder so I can easily flip

Public displays of learning are a powerful tool in the classroom to further the connection between how student learning is meaningful and important to the world around them.

#DiveintoInquiry

to any student's proposal and check in with him from day to day. I have found this method super helpful in keeping all of the Free Inquiry projects organised so I can best support each and every student in class. Imagine having thirty students learning about thirty different topics with thirty different authentic pieces. This can lead to a dizzying organisational mess. By having a strong plan outlined from the onset and a method by which I can seamlessly check in with each student day to day, I can make sense of the amount of personalisation we are aiming for in the course.

10

Explore and Research

During the Explore and Research step in the Free Inquiry Process, students actively retrieve and process information about their essential question. Depending on their inquiry focus, students seek answers to their essential question from a variety of sources. Some of these sources—literature, textbooks, films, and teachers—are traditional and familiar to the students. However, some of these sources will be unique, new to our practice, or ones students have not been encouraged to explore in previous classroom experiences. For example, interviewing professionals, calling on other teachers or experts for support, or actively seeking answers online via social media, forums, and online communities are less traditional resources.

Exploration can be an emotional research rollercoaster for students. They will likely feel overwhelmed when faced with the endless number of resources and research possibilities they can access. To help ease their concerns, I frontload the Explore and Research step by highlighting some of the challenges and emotions they will encounter during their research. Additionally, I provide them with several tips to support them on this path:

Take time to explore.

Often students begin their inquiry with a vision of what they want to learn and where they want to go. But this plan won't allow them time or freedom to stray from their inquiry topic and see other amazing opportunities or excellent resources. I ask all my students to keep an open mind, take a step back, review what they're unpacking, and honour where their research may lead them.

Be flexible about what you expect from your time.

Students expect to find some of the most important information to answer their essential question during their first research session. Not only is this unrealistic, it doesn't foster the deep research skills I want my students to gain from this process. So I encourage students to let go of what they hope to discover and, instead, settle into the process of exploring and researching.

Take time to reflect and relax.

This is an incredibly valuable tip to reinforce early and throughout the Explore and Research step of the Free Inquiry unit. Reflecting provides students with perspective, especially when it's done in groups, as a class, or in our one-on-one discussions. I encourage students to reflect on their research, their feelings, and their inquiry direction. And this is where relaxing comes in. Students may feel frustrated by the slow progress being made. They may be confused by how information is presented in different sources or feel uncertain about how their research is related to their inquiry. I assure my students these feelings are normal, and I validate them by listening to students and providing support where necessary. I try my best to keep them off the emotional research rollercoaster whilst keeping them relatively calm and focused.

USING AN INQUIRY JOURNAL

To build on these tips and best support this highly personalised research experience, I recommend students work under a common structure to help them stay organised and deepen their understanding of their essential question. This will also help you keep track of student progress and know how to best meet their needs each step of the way.

One common structure I have students include—regardless of what essential questions or authentic pieces they have selected—is learning evidence. As noted previously, learning evidence aids in the retrieval of information (note taking, summarising, or creating an outline or storyboard) and processing of information (journaling, asking questions from notes, and making inferences and connections to broaden understanding). Students can select the best methods for their learning style whilst ensuring their authentic piece is something they are proud of. See the table in chapter nine for more ideas.

An Inquiry Journal is a great tool we use throughout the year to support the processing of information. It's a place where students can make connections in their learning, ask questions, synthesise sources, highlight or collate big ideas, record brainstorms and epiphanies, and narrate their feelings during their inquiry. These activities reveal how the learning evidence that aids retrieval of information merely skims the surface of the potential to deepen their understanding of their essential question. The Inquiry Journal is where they begin to freely mash up everything they have located and start to make sense of it in their own minds.

The Inquiry Journal is where they begin to freely mash up everything they have located and start to make sense of it in their own minds.

#DiveintoInquiry

I love the Inquiry Journal process because it takes *me* deeper into understanding their inquiry. At times, I ask them to turn these in so I can look at their thoughts; other times I may ask them to reference their Inquiry Journal in a small group or one-on-one meeting. The Inquiry Journal is a place where students can voice their feelings during their inquiry—the ups and downs they encounter, moments of elation from discovery, and moments of frustration from dead ends or fruitless leads. Their Inquiry Journal makes me privy to these feelings and allows me to provide the level of support each student requires to be successful in their inquiry.

To aid the Inquiry Journal process, I will occasionally provide the entire class with a prompt so I can attain specific feedback on how their inquiry is unfolding. Prompts I've used include the following:

- What is a source of information you have found valuable in answering your essential question? How has it proved valuable?
- Reflect on your essential question and how your understanding is changing, becoming more focused, or is perhaps being reaffirmed in your research.
- Describe the ups and downs you have encountered to date in your inquiry. Specifically, when you were frustrated or struggling in your inquiry, what did you do to address the situation?
- Take a moment to reflect on your inquiry plan (calendar). Do you need to make any revisions to this plan? If so, why? If you haven't made any changes to your plan, why do you feel you have been so successful sticking to it?
- Related to your learning evidence, what have you done to make retrieving information easier?
- Knowing what you know now, what advice would you give yourself at the start of your inquiry?

Learning Evidence Check-Ins

Regardless of the kind of learning evidence students are documenting, be it retrieval or processing, frequent learning evidence check-ins are super valuable for best supporting students in their Free Inquiry unit. During the Explore and Research step in our Inquiry Process, I meet with each student a few times every week to look at their learning evidence and assess a few things.

I start by ensuring students are keeping their information organised. Source citations, headings, page numbers, and big ideas should surface from their learning. Some students create learning evidence notebooks to record everything from the inquiry and keep it in one safe place. I encourage them to take this a step further by using Google Docs to stay organised, maximise workflow, and collaborate when desired. This also allows them to seamlessly document, curate, and save any online sources they have discovered. They can then share this learning with me, and I can check in from time to time to see how they're progressing. Whatever the means, my first priority is to ensure learning evidence is organised and neat.

Next, I look for connections to their essential question and whether or not they are finding answers to deepen their understanding of their inquiry topic. I ask them to tell me what they've learned so far about their essential question. I ask them whether they feel they've made progress in their inquiry, and I hand them their proposal calendar and ask whether they're on track or need to make revisions to their plan.

Lastly, I ask them how they're feeling about the inquiry process. As you can see, my focus on their learning evidence has now shifted to the processing of their learning and their reflections on their progress.

I get a pretty good sense from these meetings about who requires support and to what extent. Upon completion of the unit, many students realise these frequent check-ins really helped them to both identify areas to explore and find solutions to challenges they were facing. Spending just a few minutes each day is all it may take, and I often find the time for these check-ins when students are actively researching and documenting their learning.

When I'm meeting with students and assessing their learning evidence, I do not give it a mark. I record I had a successful meeting and whether or not I feel each student is on track in his or her inquiry, but I do not give each student any sort of mark or percentage based on what I see. Instead, I look for meaning in their learning evidence and ask myself if they are making ground on answering their essential question. I determine if the sources of information students are unpacking are reliable, valid, and worthy of their time. I provide specific feedback to each student related to the depth of their learning evidence, the connections in their journaling, and the questions they are asking. While this was incredibly challenging for me when I first began this process in our classroom, I found providing specific, meaningful, and clear feedback throughout the Explore and Research process of our inquiry led students to feel supported. Additionally, it helped them get and stay on track and locate helpful information in answering their essential question.

COLLABORATE WITH YOUR TEACHER LIBRARIAN

My collaboration with our teacher librarian at our school has always been a crucial component of the Explore and Research step of our inquiry. I cannot overstate the power of this partnership. Today's library is unlike the one I grew up exploring. Gone are card catalogues and Dewey Decimal Systems. Plus there are fewer hard resources to leaf through. Today's library is a learning commons—one where collaboration is encouraged, support in accessing information online is the norm, and where students can learn the invaluable skill of proficient research.

Today's library is a learning commons—one where collaboration is encouraged, support in accessing information online is the norm, and where students can learn the invaluable skill of proficient research.

#DiveintoInquiry

Since I co-plan portions of our Types of Student Inquiry units with our teacher librarian, we visit our library throughout the year. Together, we identify several key skills we want our students to possess by the time they graduate and leave our school. We want students to be able to do the following:

- locate resources online and use school databases
- glean information from browsing, scanning, and skimming resources
- test a source for accuracy, objectivity, and relevance
- define the difference between academic journals, scholarly journals, and articles
- define *peer reviewed*
- cite online sources and create a reference list
- distinguish between scholarly and popular sources

In addition to helping students acquire these skills, our teacher librarian is a great partner in student-led inquiry during the Free Inquiry unit. The more I include our teacher librarian in my planning and preparation, the more support he is able to lend. Whether checking on a student's learning evidence, sharing a newly discovered

Your teacher librarian is an inquiry ally.

#DiveintoInquiry

resource to support an essential question, or helping address specific questions or challenges students are facing, our teacher librarian is an inquiry ally. By the time their Free Inquiry unit is being planned, students feel comfortable in our library and working with our teacher librarian. They freely seek his support when needed, as they know they have someone at school besides me who understands the Types of Student Inquiry and our Free Inquiry process.

11

Creating the Authentic Piece

Perhaps the most meaningful step for students in the Free Inquiry process is creating something to reflect their understanding of their essential question. I love this time. If scaffolded properly using the Types of Student Inquiry, the tenets of Understanding by Design, and a strongly structured and supported Free Inquiry unit, students' authentic pieces inspire and resonate. I keep them for years and share them with students preparing for their own Free Inquiry unit, colleagues considering initiating an inquiry process in their own classroom, on social media, and with my Personal Learning Network ("PLN") on Twitter, or at workshops and conferences across the continent.

Authentic pieces inspire and resonate. I keep them for years and share them often.

#DiveintoInquiry

Authentic pieces begin with students genuinely deciding how they want to demonstrate their understanding. I ask them, "If you could demonstrate your understanding in any way, what would it be? Are you really good at something you feel would help communicate your understanding of your essential question?" Inevitably, these questions lead students to consider authentic pieces to simultaneously reflect their learning and engage an audience.

I always ask students to connect their authentic piece to the learning standards of our course. Their piece must summarise their learning and reflect, to an extent, the must-know content our course demands. In my English classes, this can look like a personal narrative essay. In science classes, it might look like following the scientific method. In social studies classes, it can be an essential question explored through a specific time period or historical event. In math classes, it can look like mathematical problem solving, strategies, and equations from the course curriculum.

Regardless of what students design for their authentic piece, they must abide by these criteria. I assess this requirement is met during the one-on-one meeting I have with each student when I review their proposal and look for evidence that their authentic piece fits into the learning objectives of the course.

When I have seen inquiry fall short, it's due, in part, to the gap between the voice and choice provided to students and the course curriculum and learning standards of the grade level. By ensuring their Free Inquiry unit and, more specifically, their performance task (*i.e.*, authentic piece) is up to this standard, I am closing this gap.

Throughout their Free Inquiry unit, students are gathering learning evidence to scaffold the creation of this authentic piece. Now it is time to put it all together. I ask students to complete a few tasks to help guide them to a successful performance task and deepen their understanding of their essential question.

Task #1: Co-construct criteria for the authentic piece.

Shortly after students meet with me to pitch their proposal, we spend time co-constructing criteria for their authentic piece. Clearly, student ownership over their learning witnessed during our school year is powerful, but I believe when we include student self-assessment of their learning, we take this agency to another level.

> When we include self-assessment of their learning, we take student agency to another level.
>
> #DiveintoInquiry

When students can build the assessment piece of the performance task, they are more easily able to recognise how to make improvements and revisions to their work. Further, I find students are more likely to achieve a performance task they are happy with—one meeting or exceeding the criteria we've built—because creating it gives them a clear and deep understanding of how to do well. Prior to their learning being published, I ask students to self-assess their authentic piece using this co-constructed criteria. During this process, I witness students revising and enhancing their authentic piece in powerful ways. The pride they take in their learning and the attention to detail they demonstrate when self-assessing is something that cannot be replicated in any other assessment strategy.

Co-constructing criteria seems daunting. With close to thirty students in a single class working on potentially unique, authentic pieces, the hesitancy of some educators to open up their classrooms to Free Inquiry is understandable. But by the time we get to our Free Inquiry unit, students are well prepared for the responsibility and ownership of their learning. Plus, I utilise some methods to help me best meet the needs of my students.

Don't start from scratch.

Likely, the authentic piece a student has decided to create to demonstrate their understanding has been previously created and assessed by someone else. As such, I always encourage my students to find pre-existing criteria—close to what students want to create—to get the conversation started. We research and narrow our scope to a few final rubrics students feel could lend powerful language, a strong scope, and solid sequencing to assessing their authentic piece. I then ask them to revise what they've found, taking out what doesn't quite fit with their vision and adding missing details. The end result is a working draft of criteria students may decide to use to self-assess their authentic piece.

Look at other people's work and take note of what you want.

I absolutely love asking students to show me the "gold standard" of their authentic piece. I challenge them to find examples of work they deem to be professional quality. We then discuss the work in detail through a few discussion prompts. I ask students the following questions:

- What sets this work apart from others?
- What are five specific, exceptionally executed details?
- How do you want to emulate the example you found?
- What challenges do you foresee in achieving an authentic piece of similar quality?

With these reflections in mind, we revisit the working draft and add any powerful language or details students feel is necessary in their criteria.

INCLUDE THE PROFESSIONALS

A pivotal step in co-constructing criteria is calling in the professionals. I ask that students take the gold standard idea a bit further and visit someone they feel can provide professional insight into what makes an exceptional, authentic piece. For example, a student creating a photo journal as their authentic piece should consult a photographer. A student creating a painting should consult a painter or an artist. Remember Ethan and his Bazoo? Ethan consulted a mechanic and our auto shop teacher. The collaboration between the student and professional provides an eye for detail that might escape the student alone and adds powerful language or detail to the student's draft criteria.

> The collaboration between the student and professional provides an eye for detail that might escape the student alone.
>
> #DiveintoInquiry

I may also ask students to have a professional assist in the assessment of the authentic piece. There have been times in my career when I have been genuinely challenged when assessing particular authentic pieces. How do I assess the above photo journal, painting, or Bazoo? In such cases, we have included the professional in the assessment. Inevitably, the assessment process becomes a collaborative process, one attaining a holistic—yet exceptionally detailed—reflection of the quality of the authentic piece the student has produced.

Compare with the assessment standard in the course.

Throughout our course, I have used the method of co-constructing criteria with my students, and we have built a consistent language to help us assess our learning and our performance task. When it's time to co-construct criteria for the authentic pieces, I encourage students to revisit this language and the learning we've done during the year. Students review the language we've used in previous units and reflect on whether this language can help their assessment of their authentic piece. These methods combine to create a strongly scaffolded, focused, and clear criteria tool to help us assess for learning.

Task #2: Step back and review your learning evidence.

At this point, I encourage students to step away from the incredible learning they've done in their Free Inquiry unit and review their learning evidence from start to finish. I ask them to look for the key points they'd like to communicate to their audience and find those *aha* moments in their research. And I ask them to identify where the big idea of their essential question comes to the surface. These details help them decide what needs to come across to their audience in their authentic piece.

Task #3: Self-assess and revise as you go.

Using the co-designed criteria we have built for their performance task and asking themselves a few reflection questions, students self-assess as they build their authentic piece.

- *Am I on track to achieve a performance task with which I will be happy?*
- *Is my learning meeting or exceeding the expectations I've set out for myself? How can I tell?*
- *What, in my view, can I change to make my authentic piece better?*
- *What are three steps I can take to make my authentic piece awesome?*

Since students are actively *creating* their authentic piece, the criteria cannot holistically assess their learning yet. However, they can prompt students to reflect where they currently are with their authentic piece, where they need to be in the coming days of the unit, and then plan backward to ensure they close the gap between the two.

Task #4: Hook your audience on what you have learned.

I ask students to keep in mind the energy they originally felt when planning their inquiry—whether it was their passionate drive, their aim for a goal, their will to take on a new challenge, or their unceasing curiosity—and remember their audience needs to feel this as well. Essential questions and their Free Inquiry unit plan are both highly meaningful to each student. We don't, however, want this meaning and zest for learning to be lost in an authentic piece with no hook for the audience.

Task #5: Get other people's eyes on your learning.

For some students, this is the first time their learning is being shared with someone outside of our classroom, and it's a huge and awesome step for them in the creation of the authentic piece. Prying open the door to the classroom it allows others to see the learning taking place

> Prying open the door to the classroom allows others to see the learning taking place in their Free Inquiry unit.
>
> #DiveintoInquiry

in their Free Inquiry unit. It also reflects a hurdle they all face when getting prepared to publicly display their learning, and it allows students to test run whether their efforts to hook their audience are successful. I encourage students to ask their audience these questions:

- Does my learning hook you? If so, how?
- What about it resonates or is powerful?

These conversations inevitably provide highly meaningful, specific feedback and direction for completing their authentic piece.

Task #6: Have an eye on the details.

I encourage all students to create a slick, professional, and innovative authentic piece. When discussing the authentic piece, these are great adjectives to use because they inevitably lead to rich discussions about assessing *how* a performance task meets these criteria. What makes one authentic piece slick may be something entirely different from what makes another slick. For example, students creating a video to summarise their learning might use *slick, professional,* and *innovative* to describe transitions or the sharpness of images or the innovative use of the platform with which they're working. On the other hand, students creating a public presentation of their learning may use those adjectives to mean giving attention to pacing and enunciation, playing with emphasis on words and body language, and overall presence and energy. These discussions about putting the final touches on their authentic pieces always lead to polished performance tasks and an end result students will be proud of.

When students effectively complete these six tasks, their effort is reflected in an outstanding authentic piece. For example, Julia chose to create a video using *VideoScribe* to reflect her understanding of Shakespeare's *Macbeth* from our Guided Inquiry unit. She wanted to answer the essential question, *How can ambition be both a good and bad trait?*

Julia's authentic piece can be viewed here:

Another fantastic example comes from Chantaille. Chantaille chose to create a video using *Explain Everything* to reflect her understanding of a *science humaines* class (French immersion social studies) from our Guided Inquiry unit focusing on comparing and contrasting Victorian-era values with present day contemporary values. She used her understanding to answer the essential question, *How can we learn from the past to understand the present world?*

Take a look at Chantaille's authentic piece here:

These examples, as well as others shared throughout this book, demonstrate how student understanding can be shared to an authentic audience whilst also meeting the learning standards of a specific course. Combined with a first person narrative account of how their essential question is meaningful to them, what they learned about their essential question throughout their Free Inquiry unit, and what challenged them along the way, the authentic piece is the culmination of our scaffolding through the Types of Student Inquiry.

12

Public Display of Understanding

Upon completion of their Free Inquiry unit, students share their learning in what I call the Public Display of Understanding. This is the climax of our course and the culmination of everything they have learned about the Types of Student Inquiry, Understanding by Design, and their essential question. Students share their authentic piece and see the impact their inquiry has on others.

While I facilitate this Public Display of Understanding in a number of ways, I always begin with sharing inquiry within our class and school. Sharing with our own learning community first has an amazing effect on everyone in the building. When other students and teachers see how inquiry can lead to powerful authentic pieces and a meaningful and relevant connection to learning, they can't help but want to get in on the fun. By displaying our Free Inquiry authentic pieces to our school, we make a great impact toward changing our educational landscape.

> By displaying our learning to our school, we make a great impact toward changing our educational landscape.

#DiveintoInquiry

One way I support students sharing their learning with our school is by organizing an Inquiry Open House. We set up inquiry stations in a large space in our school such as the library, open foyer, gymnasium, or cafeteria. We then invite all classes and any student-selected guests to attend during a particular time in the day. We share with them our authentic pieces and an overview of our Free Inquiry unit.

The format for the audience is similar to speed dating: Groups of three to five visit each station, and my students have ten minutes to share their inquiry to this audience. I keep time and cue the audience to transition to their next inquiry station when the ten minutes is up. This format is great. Presenters get to refine their sharing with each round. The smaller groups provide a certain level of ease and confidence for the presenter, and the audience gets to hear about several inquiry projects in a relatively short period of time.

Another way I have supported students sharing their learning in our school is through an Inquiry Gallery Walk. I love when students can display their authentic piece over an extended period of time so an audience can view it and interact with it. In this venue, the emphasis shifts from the student doing the talking to the authentic piece itself speaking to the audience. This format challenges students to create an installation or visual representation to hook their audience and pull them in for a closer inspection of their Free Inquiry unit.

> I love when students can display their authentic piece over an extended period of time so an audience can view it and interact with it.
>
> #DiveintoInquiry

Our Inquiry Gallery Walks typically consist of three components: First, students must display a visual representation of their authentic piece. Most often students hang a large photograph (I suggest eleven by fourteen inches) of their authentic piece; however, if the authentic piece allows, some students actually display an installation or physical manifestation of their learning. I try to display these artifacts of learning in a single space in the school. Hallways, corridors, or a learning space work well to allow a start and end point for our audience.

Second, accompanying the visual representation of learning is an inquiry statement written by the student. Students use the first section from their proposal (where I asked students, "What is your essential question?") to write their statement. Their reflection on those initial questions informs the audience of the background of their inquiry and the underlying motivation for exploring their essential question. Students display this inquiry statement underneath the visual representation in our Inquiry Gallery Walk.

Finally, each student creates a short video describing their Free Inquiry unit and demonstrating their understanding of their essential question. *Explain Everything* is a great app allowing students to annotate and narrate images, documents, and video. In fact, many of my students opt to use this platform to create a five-minute inquiry-reflection video. We then publish the video to a class YouTube channel and create a QR code to accompany our installation.

The visual representation, inquiry statement, and QR code and video combine to create an interactive inquiry display that audiences can visit for an extended time. In fact, we have had many of our Inquiry Gallery Walks on display throughout and beyond the school year. Students get excited when they catch someone standing in front of their work and watching their video on a device. This authentic connection—one highlighting the relationship between what they've learned and the world around them—is powerful stuff.

It's important to note that not all Free Inquiry units need to be displayed to such a broad audience. I have worked with many introverted students who have planned and executed exceptionally strong Free Inquiry units, create amazing authentic pieces, but shy away from sharing their learning with others. Our Inquiry Open House and the Inquiry Gallery Walk can be too much for some students to face; therefore, I always host a class-sharing of their Free Inquiry units, which we call Inquiry Rounds. Inquiry Rounds are similar in format to our Inquiry Open House but are scaled down in scope so only our immediate class participates. Students share their Free Inquiry unit to two audience members for a ten-minute period before I cue the groups to transition to another station. Inquiry Rounds can scaffold toward the Inquiry Open House or serve as a complete substitution for the more introverted students.

Many authentic pieces lend well to a public display of understanding to share beyond our school community. Depending on the nature of the essential question and the student's reason for exploring their inquiry topic, I may encourage some students to display specific authentic pieces for specific audiences. One of my students created a video game reflecting a historical event for a social studies class, and I encouraged the student to take her authentic piece to a gaming expo. Another student created an Instagram account of portraits and interviews of students from our school, all answering the question, *What makes our school awesome?* This social media account was then shared to classes at local elementary and middle schools as an example of how social media can be used responsibly and meaningfully.

> Publicly sharing students' learning with other students demonstrates to them how their work in school is more than just "work in school."
>
> #DiveintoInquiry

Publicly sharing students' learning with other students demonstrates to them how their work in school is more than just "work in school." This culminating step in our journey through inquiry is a celebration of their commitment to doing things differently in their education. From the onset of our course, I challenge students to go down a different path—one calling on them to be active in their learning, accountable for their role in their education, and brave in the face of a new and unknown process. This Public Display of Understanding completes our journey in the course and concludes their Free Inquiry unit.

13

Conclusion

At the start of this book, I proposed that you move forward in your reading and adopting of inquiry with three things in mind: First, I encourage you to think big and plan for the future classroom you want for your learners.

If, in two to three years, you wish to have adopted inquiry into your classroom one hundred percent of the time, you can begin to chip away at this transition right now by moving on to my second piece of advice: Start with small changes first. Maybe you start by co-designing your course outline with your students to empower their role in their learning. Or perhaps you begin to critique inquiry to gauge student excitement or concern over entering into an inquiry model. Or perhaps you revise an awesome unit of study of your own to reflect a Structured Inquiry approach. Whatever you do, take small steps at first and reflect and revise as you go.

Lastly, always keep your learners at the heart of inquiry. Think of them as you plan what inquiry will look like in your own classroom. Consider how they will respond to being given more agency over their learning. Question how you can best meet the needs of the learners with whom you collaborate.

And now I'd like to add a fourth item to this list: Find comfort in the mess of uncertainty. As you try inquiry on for size and begin to shift control of learning in your classroom from you to your students, be prepared for not knowing exactly how things will turn out. Counter this by spending time in class having conversations with your students

Find comfort in the mess of uncertainty.

#DiveintoInquiry

to assess for understanding. Reflect on what each of your learners needs from you and provide it for them. Know that, in order to see results you have never seen, you will need to do things you've never done.

We are incredibly fortunate to be educators. Working alongside the innovators of tomorrow and encouraging them to take agency and risks in their learning is such a gift. It is one I cherish dearly and take advantage of daily. I challenge you to do the same. Make your relationships count, and dive into inquiry!

Thank you for allowing me to share my journey with you.

References

Alberta Learning: Learning and Teaching Resources Branch, *Focus on Inquiry* (Alberta Learning Resource Centre, 2004).

McTighe, Jay and Grant Wiggins, *Understanding by Design* (Association for Supervision and Curriculum Development, 2005).

Rothstein, Dan and Santana, Luz, *Make Just One Change: Teaching Students to Ask Their Own Questions* (Harvard Education Press, 2011).

Acknowledgments

I'd like to express my utmost thanks and sincere gratitude to the following people who have unceasingly encouraged and supported me over the years; My parents—all of them—for their unconditional love and sacrifices; Susan, Jeremy, and the rest of the Tate line for being the scaffolding for our family; The Dupres and Lejbaks for taking me in, letting me stick around, and sharing many years of friendship; And to my own teachers and coaches who, during turbulent times, never gave up and always believed in me—even when I didn't believe in myself.

A number of close friends have also supported my growth as an educator, and I cannot thank each of you enough. My thanks go to the following: My mentors, Bryn Barker and Jim Wallace, for showing me the ropes at Esquimalt and teaching me the meaning of the word *dedication*; My good friends, Ken Henderson, Jonathan Schneider, and Will Moore, for encouraging me to take risks and make them count; My number one resource (and a teacher's best friend), Geoff Orme, for sharing my passion for inquiry, for always having a chair for me when I needed it, and for the endless guidance and advice; Colin Roberts, for gently nurturing questions and providing ways to explore them in my classroom; My critical friends, Petra Eggert and Dave Shortreed, for showing me how to best support student learning and deepen understanding; To the ever courageous and innovative Rebecca Bathurst-Hunt for bringing my vision to life and being such an amazing educator; To Alec Couros for his vision and voice, and for crafting such a compelling forward to this book; To Holly Clark for entering my classroom and planting a seed that I've seen grow into something powerfully special; and to my Esquimalt family, *"Hay'sxw'qa!"* and *"Esse quam videri."*

Lastly, my thanks go to the many students whom I have been blessed to know over the years: the Esquimalt, the Songhees, the Dockers, and the Bays. Whether you know it or not, you made your mark on me, and I am forever thankful. Without you, this book could not have been possible.

Are You Ready to Dive into Inquiry?

Here are ways to stay connected:

1. Host a Workshop at Your School
   - **Dive into Inquiry Workshop**—Create and Customize Learning for Your Classroom (one-day).
   - **Engage Me!**—Learn how to Transition into Inquiry (half-day).
   - **Private Label**—Trevor MacKenzie will customize a workshop to fit your school's needs.

2. Take the Online Course:
   - Dive into Inquiry BootCamp

3. Attend an EdTechTeam Summit in your area featuring Google for Education.
4. Schedule Trevor for a Dive into Inquiry Keynote

For more information visit EdTechTeam.com/press

To request a workshop or for more info contact press@edtechteam.com

TrevorMacKenzie.com | #DiveintoInquiry

More Books from EdTechTeam Press
edtechteam.com/books

THE HYPERDOC HANDBOOK
Digital Lesson Design Using Google Apps
By Lisa Highfill, Kelly Hilton, and Sarah Landis

The HyperDoc Handbook is a practical reference guide for all K–12 educators who want to transform their teaching into blended-learning environments. This bestselling book strikes the perfect balance between pedagogy and how-to tips while also providing ready-to-use lesson plans to get you started with HyperDocs right away.

INNOVATE WITH iPAD
Lessons to Transform Learning in the Classroom
By Karen Lirenman and Kristen Wideen

Written by two primary teachers, *Innovate with iPad* provides a complete selection of clearly explained, engaging, open-ended lessons to change the way you use iPad in the classroom. It features downloadable task cards, student-created examples, and extension ideas to use with your students. Whether you have access to one iPad for your entire class or one for each student, these lessons will help you transform learning in your classroom.

ASSESSMENT THAT MATTERS
Using Technology to Personalize Learning
By Kim Meldrum

In *Assessment That Matters,* Kim Meldrum explains the three types of assessment—assessment *as* learning, assessment *for* learning, and assessment *of* learning. Within her instruction on gathering rich assessment information, you'll find simple strategies and tips for using today's technology to allow students to demonstrate learning in creative and innovative ways.

THE SPACE
A Guide for Educators
By Rebecca Louise Hare and Robert Dillon

The Space takes the current conversation about reshaping school spaces to the next level. This book goes well beyond the ideas for learning-space design that focus on Pinterest-perfect classrooms and instead discusses real and practical ways to design learning spaces that support and drive learning.

A LEARNER'S PARADISE
How New Zealand Is Reimagining Education
By Richard Wells

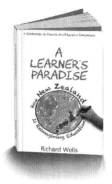

What if teachers were truly trusted to run education? In *A Learner's Paradise*, Richard Wells describes New Zealand's forward-thinking education system in which teachers are empowered to do exactly that. With no prescribed curriculum, teachers and students work together to create individualized learning plans—all the way through the high school level. From this guidebook, you'll learn how New Zealand is reimagining education and setting an example for innovative educators, parents, and school districts everywhere to follow.

THE GOOGLE APPS GUIDEBOOK
Lessons, Activities, and Projects Created by Students for Teachers
By Kern Kelley and the Tech Sherpas

The Google Apps Guidebook is filled with great ideas for the classroom from the voice of the students themselves. Each chapter introduces an engaging project that teaches students (and teachers) how to use one of Google's powerful tools. Projects are differentiated for a variety of age ranges and can be adapted for most content areas.

CLASSROOM MANAGEMENT IN THE DIGITAL AGE

Effective Practices for Technology-Rich Learning Spaces

By Patrick Green and Heather Dowd

Classroom Management in the Digital Age helps guide and support teachers through the new landscape of device-rich classrooms. It provides practical strategies to novice and expert educators alike who want to maximize learning and minimize distraction. Learn how to keep up with the times while limiting time wasters and senseless screen-staring.

Sign up to learn more about new and upcoming books at bit.ly/edtechteambooks

About the Author

Trevor MacKenzie loves drinking good coffee, riding bikes, wrestling with his two sons, Ewan and Gregor, eating food, and all other things lovely in life. He actually *does* enjoy long walks on the beach, as he and his family reside in beautiful Victoria, British Columbia, Canada.

Trevor only has two regrets in life: When he proposed to his wife, Sarah, he didn't have a ring and hadn't asked for her father's blessing of their marriage. Internally, he has been living this down ever since and making up for it by showering his family with ice cream, mowing the yard, and love.

Trevor attended the University of Victoria where he tried to play varsity basketball. Having never seen a shot he didn't like, he only played a single season. He graduated with a degree in English and geography and completed his teaching certification in 2004. He is currently a teacher at Oak Bay High School. Additionally, he is a graduate student at the University of Victoria, researching the impact of growing student agency afforded by an inquiry-based learning pedagogical model on student's self-efficacy under the tutelage of Dr. Valerie Irvine.

Made in the USA
Charleston, SC
06 December 2016